The Little Book
of

LOVE

The Little Book
of
LOVE

Edited by

Joules Taylor and Esme Hawes

BARNES
&NOBLE
BOOKS
NEW YORK

This edition published by Barnes & Noble Inc,
by arrangement with Parragon

2003 Barnes & Noble Books
Copyright © Parragon 2001

This book was created by Magpie Books,
an imprint of Constable & Robinson Ltd

Cover illustration courtesy of Photodisc Europe
Cover design Simon Levy

10 9 8 7 6 5 4 3 2

ISBN 0-7607-3778-9

A copy of the British Library Cataloguing-in-Publication Data
is available from the British Library

Printed in China

Contents

Introduction

So much has been written about love, through the ages. It's the most mysterious of all feelings, difficult to understand, impossible to control, at the same time the most fragile and powerful of emotions. From the warm, tender bond between parent and child, to the strong, staunch and mellow love of couples who have spent their lives together, we can't live without it! Included in this little book are some of the great poems that most successfully capture this universal feeling of love.

But sometimes things don't go quite according to plan: occasionally a little help — a little magic — is needed to smooth the way and create happiness where there was sorrow. That's where this book is intended to help.

Magic is nothing more, or less, than making things happen — purely through the power of your will. Some people are able to do this within themselves, while others need an external object — a talisman or amulet — as a *focus. Some prefer a spoken charm, or the emotional satisfaction of a full ritual designed to enhance romantic potential. You will find all of this and more in this book, and we wish you good luck in your search for love and happiness. However, it is wise to remember the greatest charm of all – to be charming!*

Live With Me

~

Live with me, and be my love,
And we will all the pleasure prove
That hills and valleys, dales and fields,
And all the craggy mountains yields.

There will we sit upon the rocks,
And see the shepherds feed their flocks
By shallow rivers, by whose falls
Melodious birds sing madrigals.

There will I make thee a bed of roses,
With a thousand fragrant posies,
A cap of flowers, and a kirtle
Embroider'd all with leaves of myrtle.

A belt of straw and ivy buds
With coral clasps and amber studs,
And if these pleasures may thee move,
Then live with me and be my love.

Anon   16th century

Chapter 1

~❦~

FLOWER MAGIC

Just about everyone knows that a red rose is a symbol of love — but did you know that most other flowers — and some fruits — also carry hidden meanings?

Although little used today, a complete "Language of Flowers" was devised during the last 150 years, allowing lovers to send secret messages to each other. In the following pages you'll learn how to tell your beloved how you feel about them, and how they feel about you! Learn this magical language, and let flower spells work for you . . .

FIRST ATTEMPTS...

~

There are some delightful ways to flirt using flowers —
though you need to be careful to use the right ones!
And it's not necessary to spend a fortune at the florist:
a lot of common garden plants or wildflowers have
their own meanings too. (But you should always be
wary of the color yellow when sending flowers...).

On first meeting someone who makes your heart
miss a beat, try giving them a red carnation — it means
"Ah! my poor heart — I am smitten!"

You could hope to receive a cheerful bunch of
celandines in return — they symbolize "pleasures and
happiness to come," while the simple garden daisy
indicates that the giver shares your feelings.

But a striped carnation means, "I refuse your
advances," while a yellow indicates that the object of
your affection holds you in disdain: depending on the
strength of your feelings, it might be better to try
elsewhere. And if you are given basil, you'd better give
up altogether — it might be the king of herbs, but in
the language of flowers it means, "I hate you!"

However, a single white rosebud is a hopeful sign: it

means that the giver's heart is innocent and hasn't yet known love. Perhaps you are the person to teach them its joys . . .

First Love

I ne'er was struck before that hour
With love so sudden and so sweet
Her face it bloomed like a sweet flower
And stole my heart away complete
My face turned pale a deadly pale
My legs refused to walk away
And when she looked what could I ail
My life and all seemed turned to clay

And then my blood rushed to my face
And took my eyesight quite away
The trees and bushes round the place
Seemed midnight at noon day
I could not see a single thing
Words from my eyes did start
They spoke as chords do from the string
And blood burnt round my heart

Are flowers the winter's choice
Is love's bed always snow
She seemed to hear my silent voice
Not loves appeals to know
I never saw so sweet a face
As that I stood before
My heart has left its dwelling place
And can return no more –

John Clare 1793–1864

TREES AND SHRUBS

~

There are quite a few trees and shrubs to choose from
if you want to let your beloved know which of their
qualities you admire.

A spray of elm leaves symbolizes dignity, while the
rowan represents prudence.

A birch twig symbolizes meekness, and a spray
from the black poplar says that you delight in their
courageous spirit. A sprig of holly means you admire
their foresight, while larch leaves let them know you
think them bold and audacious!

Leaves from the beech tree symbolize riches, and
can be seen as a lucky charm if exchanged between
lovers. A twig from the box tree suggests that you will
be stoical and staunch in your love, regardless of how
the   other   responds,   while   a   cedar   twig
symbolizes strength and enduring love.

A sprig from the elder tree tells your lover that you
are zealous in your feelings — but be wary of giving
sweet-scented linden flowers: they symbolize conjugal
love and could be taken as a proposal of marriage!

Lilac, that lovely, fragrant, flowering shrub, sends

several messages. White lilac expresses the innocence of youth; the mauve or light purple lilac symbolizes young love, while the deep purple variety may be exchanged between lovers in a long-term relationship to reaffirm their love.

There are also ways to let your beloved know you love them for their mind! Clematis sends the message, "your mind and imagination are beautiful," while a single dahlia indicates that you think they have excellent taste! Laburnum flowers tell your beloved they are a pensive beauty — but make sure they aren't wilted: dying laburnum flowers mean you feel yourself forsaken and hopeless in love.

A Picture

~

It was in autumn that I met
Her whom I love; the sunflowers bold
Stood up like guards around her set,
And all the air with mignonette
Was warm within the garden old;
Beside her feet the marigold
Glowed star-like, and the sweet-pea sent
A sigh to follow as she went
Slowly adown the terrace; — there
I saw thee, oh my love! and thou wert fair.

She stood in the full noonday, unafraid,
As one beloved of sunlight, for awhile
She leant upon the timeworn balustrade;
The white clematis wooed her, and the clove
Hung all its burning heart upon her smile;
And on her cheek and in her eyes was love;
And on her lips that, like an opening rose,
Seemed parting some sweet secret to
   disclose,

The soul of all the summer lingered; – there
I saw thee, oh my love! and thou wert fair.
Dora Greenwell   1821–82

At a Dinner Party

~

With fruit and flowers the board is decked,
The wine and laughter flow;
I'll not complain – could one expect
So dull a world to know?

You look across the fruit and flowers,
My glance your glances find. –
It is our secret, only ours,
Since all the world is blind.

Amy Levy   1861–89

Villeggiature

My window, framed in pear-tree bloom,
White-curtained shone, and softly lighted:
So, by the pear-tree, to my room
Your ghost last night climbed uninvited.

Your solid self, long leagues away,
Deep in dull books, had hardly missed me:
And yet you found this Romeo's way,
And through the blossom climbed and
    kissed me.

I watched the still and dewy lawn,
The pear-tree boughs hung white above you:
I listened to you till the dawn,
And half forgot I did not love you.

Oh, dear! what pretty things you said,
What pearls of song you threaded for me!
I did not – till your ghost had fled –
Remember how you always bore me!

Edith Nesbit 1858–1924

The Gift

~

What can I give you, my lord, my lover,
You who have given the world to me,
Showed me the light and the joy that cover
The wild sweet earth and the restless sea?

All that I have are gifts of your giving –
If I gave them again, you would find them
    old,
And your soul would weary of always living
Before the mirror my life would hold.

What shall I give you, my lord, my lover?
The gift that breaks the heart in me:
I bid you awake at dawn and discover
I have gone my way and left you free.

Sara Teasdale 1884–1933

The Hill

~

Breathless, we flung us on the windy hill,
Laughed in the sun, and kissed the lovely grass.
You said, 'Through glory and ecstasy we pass;
Wind, sun, and earth remain, the birds sing
    still,
When we are old, are old …' 'And when we die
All's over that is ours; and life burns on
Through other lovers, other lips,' said I,
'Heart of my heart, our heaven is now, is won!'

'We are Earth's best, that learnt her lesson here.
Life is our cry. We have kept the faith!' we said;
'We shall go down with unreluctant tread
Rose-crowned into the darkness!' … Proud we
    were,
And laughed, that had such brave true things to
    say.
– And then you suddenly cried, and turned
    away.

Rupert Brooke 1887–1915

The Willing Mistress

~

Amyntas led me to a Grove,
Where all the trees did shade us;
The sun itself, though it had strove,
It could not have betray'd us:
The place secur'd from humane eyes,
No other fear allows,
But when the Winds that gently rise,
Do kiss the yielding boughs.

Down there we sat upon the moss,
And did begin to play
A thousand amorous tricks, to pass
The heat of all the day.
A many kisses he did give:
And I return'd the same
Which made me willing to receive
That which I dare not name.

His charming eyes no aid requir'd
To tell their softning tale:

On her that was already fir'd,
'Twas easy to prevail.
He did but kiss and clasp me round,
And lay'd me gently on the ground;
Ah who can guess the rest?

Aphra Behn   1640–89

HERBS AND VEGETABLES

~

While perhaps not the most apparent floral tributes, nevertheless some herbs and vegetables can express your feelings as well as a bunch of flowers – and in a less obvious fashion. So if you wish to be subtle, try some of these . . .

An ancient way to use the lovely blue flowers of borage is to float them in a glass of wine. Borage represents blunt speaking, and indicates that everything you are about to say should be taken seriously – so make sure you mean it! Rue symbolizes disdain, and rosemary remembrance: the latter may be given in memory of good times you have spent together. Sweet basil indicates "good wishes," while chervil symbolizes sincerity: in combination with sorrel ("fondness") or – even better – wood sorrel ("joy"), such a posy is a charming and heartfelt wish for good luck and happiness.

Coriander indicates that you have a secret to tell, or that there are hidden qualities under a flippant exterior. Cress represents a promise of stability, while angelica tells the other that they inspire you. Bay leaves promise that you will be faithful to the end, while fennel tells your beloved you think them worthy of everyone's praises. Sage symbolizes great esteem, while peppermint expresses the true warmth of your feelings.

Strawberry flowers express the expectation of good times ahead – raspberries symbolize remorse and may be given as an apology. Be wary of blackberries, though – they symbolize envy. Peaches are an ideal gift to receive – they mean that the giver thinks your beauty, charm and good qualities are unequalled. Cherries represent youthful vitality, while pears represent warm affection.

Sweet chestnut expresses a wish for your lover's life to be filled with luxuries, and walnuts indicate a respect for their intellect. Lemons mean, "you bring vitality to my life"; apples symbolize temptation; and the pineapple tells your beloved that you think they are perfect. Turnips represent a charitable nature, while truffles indicate a surprise in the offing; mushrooms, however, symbolize suspicion, so employ them with care. The potato symbolizes benevolence and magnanimity. Even the humble cabbage has a meaning – "we will profit from our partnership!"

Two in the Campagna

~

I wonder do you feel to-day
As I have felt, since, hand in hand,
We sat down on the grass, to stray
In spirit better through the land,
This morn of Rome and May?

For me, I touched a thought, I know,
Has tantalized me many times,
(Like turns of thread the spiders throw
Mocking across our path) for rhymes
To catch at and let go.

Help me to hold it! First it left
The yellowing fennel, run to seed
There, branching from the brickwork's
    cleft,
Some old tomb's ruin; yonder weed
Took up the floating weft,

Where one small orange cup amassed
Five beetles, — blind and green they grope
Among the honey-meal: and last,
Everywhere on the grassy slope
I traced it. Hold it fast!

The champaign with its endless fleece
Of feathery grasses everywhere!
Silence and passion, joy and peace,
An everlasting wash of air —
Rome's ghost since her decease.

Such life there, through such lengths of
    hours,
Such miracles performed in play,
Such primal naked forms of flowers,
Such letting nature have her way
While Heaven looks from its towers!

How say you? Let us, O my dove,
Let us be unashamed of soul,
As earth lies bare to heaven above!
How is it under our control
To love or not to love?

I would that you were all to me,
You that are just so much, no more.
Nor yours, nor mine, — nor slave nor free!
Where does the fault lie? What the
    core
O'the wound, since wound must be?

I would I could adopt your will,
See with your eyes, and set my heart
Beating by yours, and drink my fill
At your soul's springs, — your part, my part
In life, for good and ill.

No. I yearn upward, touch you close,
Then stand away. I kiss your cheek,
Catch your soul's warmth, — I pluck the rose
And love it more than tongue can speak —
Then the good minute goes.

Already how am I so far
Out of that minute? Must I go
Still like the thistle-ball, no bar,
Onward, whenever light winds blow,
Fixed by no friendly star?

Just when I seemed about to learn!
Where is the thread now? Off again!
The old trick! Only I discern –
Infinite passion, and the pain
Of finite hearts that yearn.

Robert Browning 1812–89

A Red, Red Rose

~

O my Love's like a red, red rose,
That's newly sprung in June;
O my Love's like the melodie
That's sweetly play'd in tune –

As fair art thou, my bonnie lass,
So deep in love am I;
And I will love thee still, my Dear,
Till a' the seas gang dry –

Till a' the seas gang dry, my Dear,
And the rocks melt wi' the sun:
I will love thee still, my Dear,
While the sands o' life shall run –

And fare thee well, my only Love!
And fare thee well, a while!
And I will come again, my Love,
Tho' it were ten thousand mile!

Robert Burns 1759–96

ROSES

～

Roses symbolize love in all its forms, and the language of roses almost deserves a book to itself! However, the following short list should enable you to pick your way through the minefield . . .

A single rose – I love you – pure and simple.

Thornless rose – I have loved you since I first saw you.

White rose – I am worthy of you. (Alternatively – You are a heavenly creature.)

Pink rose – You are graceful and elegant.

Red rose – symbolizes happy love.

Deep red rose – symbolizes bashful love, secret love.

Purple-red rose – You don't know how lovely you are!

Cream rose – Your beauty is forever new . . .

"Blue" rose – Meet me by moonlight.

Orange rose – I am infatuated with you.

Coral-colored rose – symbolizes sexual desire.

Yellow rose – I grow tired of you. (Alternatively – I am jealous.)

Red and white roses together – We are united in love.

Striped roses – We are at war.

Wild rose – The joy of loving you is mixed with pain.

Musk rose – You are beautiful but capricious. (I wish you'd make up your mind!)

"Cabbage" rose (old-fashioned variety – large with lots of petals) – Please be my love.

Opened rose in a bunch with two rosebuds – Keep our love a secret.

Single red rosebud – You are truly beautiful, the prize of my heart.

Single white rosebud – symbolizes a pure heart, one that has not yet known love.

Bouquet of rosebuds – symbolizes innocent love.

Bouquet of opened white roses and rosebuds – You are too pure and angelic for earthly love. (Not recommended for hopeful lovers!)

Song

～

Go, lovely rose –
Tell her that wastes her time and me,
That now she knows,
When I resemble her to thee
How sweet and fair she seems to be.

Tell her that's young,
And shuns to have her graces spied,
That hadst thou sprung
In deserts where no men abide,
Thou must have uncommended died.

Small is the worth
Of beauty from the light retired:
Bid her come forth,
Suffer herself to be desired,
And not blush so to be admired.

Then die! – that she
The common fate of all things rare
May read in thee;
How small a part of time they share
That are so wondrous sweet and fair!

Edmund Waller 1606–87

Sonnet 130

~

My mistress' eyes are nothing like the sun;
Coral is far more red than her lips' red:
If snow be white, why then her breasts are
    dun;
If hairs be wires, black wires grow on her
    head.
I have seen roses damask'd, red and white,
But no such roses see I in her cheeks;
And in some perfumes is there more delight
Than in the breath that from my mistress
    reeks.
I love to hear her speak, yet well I know
That music hath a far more pleasing sound:
I grant I never saw a goddess go, —
My mistress, when she walks, treads on the
    ground:
And yet, by heaven, I think my love as rare
As any she belied with false compare.

William Shakespeare 1564–1616

I Would Not Feign a Single Sigh

~

I would not feign a single sigh
Nor weep a single tear for thee,
The soul within these orbs burns dry,
A desert spreads where love should be.
I would not be a worm to crawl
A wreathing suppliant in thy way;
For love is life, is heaven, and all
The beams of an immortal day.

For sighs are idle things, and vain,
And tears for idiots vainly fall,
I would not kiss thy face again
Nor round thy shining slippers crawl.
Love is the honey, not the bee,
Nor would I turn its sweets to gall
For all the beauty found in thee,
Thy lily neck, rose cheek, and all.

I would not feign a single tale
Thy kindness or thy love to seek.

Nor sigh for Jenny of the Vale,
Her ruby smile or rosy cheek.
I would not have a pain to own
For those dark curls, and those bright eyes.
A frowning lip, a heart of stone,
False love and folly I despise.

John Clare   1793–1864

Love and Friendship

~

Love is like the wild rose-briar,
Friendship like the holly tree –
The holly is dark when the rose-briar
 blooms
But which will bloom most constantly?

The wild rose-briar is sweet in spring,
Its summer blossoms scent the air;
Yet wait till winter comes again
And who will call the wild-briar fair?

Then scorn the silly rose-wreath now
And deck thee with the holly's sheen,
That when December blights thy brow
He still may leave thy garland green.

Emily Brontë 1818–48

To the Virgins, To Make Much of Time

Gather ye rose-buds while ye may,
Old Time is still a flying:
And this same flower that smiles to-day,
Tomorrow will be dying.

The glorious lamp of heaven, the Sun,
The higher he's a getting;
The sooner will his race be run,
And nearer he's to setting.

That age is best, which is the first,
When youth and blood are warmer;
But being spent, the worse, and worst
Times, still succeed the former.

Then be not coy, but use your time;
And while ye may, go marry:
For having lost but once your prime,
You may for ever tarry.

Robert Herrick 1591–1674

FOR A MORE LIMITED BUDGET AND SIMPLER TASTES...

~

Chrysanthemums represent cheerfulness, especially in difficult times: choose red for sturdy love, or white for honesty (yellow indicates you feel yourself slighted and is probably best avoided). Lily of the valley symbolizes a return to happiness and is a charming gift to receive from a lover after you've been away. Pansies represent thoughts – blue for "I miss you," purple means "you fill my life with riches," orange symbolizes warm hugs, while the multi-colored, "face" varieties express hope that the recipient is feeling happy. Wild pansies – heartsease – symbolize "you are always in my thoughts."

White clover says, "think of me," while red clover means, "don't work too hard!": a four-leafed clover means, "please be my love."

Honeysuckle expresses admiration for the recipient's sweet disposition and a hope that love will always be true. Ivy symbolizes friendship and faithfulness; a sprig of ivy with its tendrils indicates that you are eager to please them. Lunaria (Honesty) represents truth and sincerity, as does fern; and daffodils express deep regard for the beloved.

Iris says you have a message to give your lover, but would prefer to do so in person. Enchanter's nightshade, that charming little wildflower of the woods, tells your beloved that they fascinate and bewitch you. Bluebells symbolize constant affection, and are reputed to make the bearer speak only the truth . . .

A simple dock leaf symbolizes that you will wait patiently for your love, while mistletoe, especially out of season, tells them you will overcome all difficulties to win their heart. (In season – at Yuletide – it becomes a fertility symbol, and kissing below it brings good luck.)

If your lover sends you yellow tulips ("your love has no chance of success"), try responding with stinging nettles; they symbolize, "you are too cruel." Hopefully you will receive hazelnuts – "let us be reconciled" – in return!

Of course, if you want to get a less favorable message across, there are other plants to choose.

Maple leaves indicate that the giver is unsure of the situation and would prefer to wait and see, while privet symbolizes prohibitions and denial: though useful as a hedging plant, it's not recommended for bouquets! Dead leaves symbolize melancholic sadness: the dead leaves of specific trees or shrubs indicate the death of the quality or feeling that plant represents.

Crab-apple blossom lets the recipient know you think them ill natured, while giving hops, or the gentian flower, means that you feel you have been treated unjustly. Purple hyacinth symbolizes sorrow: it can be given either to say "sorry," or to express distress at the other's behavior. If you want to be tacitly rude, you can always have a small bunch of redcurrants delivered: their message ("you please everyone") is two-edged, meaning either "everyone likes you," or something a lot less flattering!

While lavender is renowned for its healing abilities and lovely old-world fragrance, it's not overly welcome as a floral tribute – in the language of flowers it means "I don't fully trust you." Mind you, that could be useful as a warning to mend your ways! Convolvulus symbolizes uncertainty and a fear of being trapped in a relationship. And to extricate yourself from a relationship where the other is clinging, try sending sweetbrier: it means, "I wound in order to heal – I am no longer yours."

The Lost Love

~

She dwelt among the untrodden ways
Beside the springs of Dove;
A maid whom there were none to praise
And very few to love:

A violet by a mossy stone
Half-hidden from the eye!
– Fair as a star, when only one
Is shining in the sky.

She lived unknown, and few could know
When Lucy ceased to be;
But she is in her grave, and, oh,
The difference to me!

William Wordsworth 1770–1850

Carrefour

O you,
Who came upon me once
Stretched under apple-trees just after
    bathing,
Why did you not strangle me before
    speaking
Rather than fill me with the wild white
    honey of your words
And then leave me to the mercy
Of the forest bees?

Amy Lowell 1874–1925

The Knight and the Lady

~

The knight knocked at the castle gate;
The lady marvelled who was thereat.
To call the porter he would not blin;
The lady said he should not come in.

The portress was a lady bright;
Strangeness that lady hight.
She asked him what was his name;
He said, 'Desire, your man, Madame.'

She said, 'Desire, what do ye here?'
He said, 'Madame, as your prisoner.'
He was counselled to brief a bill,
And show my lady his own will.

'Kindness,' said she, 'would it bear,'
'And Pity,' said she, 'would be there.'
Thus how they did we cannot say;
We left them there and went our way.

William Cornish d. 1524

The Legend of the Forget-me-not

Forget-me-not, the lover's flower, means "I love you truly — do not forget me." The legend behind this bright blue flower's name is a delightful, if sad, tale:

A knight in armor and his lady were walking by a river when the lady spied some pretty blue flowers growing by the water. She admired them, and the knight went to pick them for her. Alas, his armor unbalanced him, and he tumbled into the water, still clutching the flowers. As he went under for the third and last time, he threw the flowers to his love, crying "Forget-me-not . . ."

(The legend doesn't say what happened to the lady. We may hope that she stayed true to his wish!)

La Belle Dame Sans Merci

O what can ail thee, knight-at-arms,
Alone and palely loitering?
The sedge has withered from the lake,
And no birds sing.

O what can ail thee, knight-at-arms,
So haggard and so woe-begone?
The squirrel's granary is full,
And the harvest's done.

I see a lily on thy brow
With anguish moist and fever-dew;
And on thy cheek a fading rose
Fast withereth too.

I met a lady in the meads,
Full beautiful – a faery's child,
Her hair was long, her foot was light,
And her eyes were wild.

I made a garland for her head,
And bracelets too, and fragrant zone;
She looked at me as she did love,
And made sweet moan.

I set her on my pacing steed
And nothing else saw all day long,
For sidelong would she bend, and sing
A faery's song.

She found me roots of relish sweet,
And honey wild and manna dew,
And sure in language strange she said –
'I love thee true'.

She took me to her elfin grot,
And there she wept and sigh'd full sore,
And there I shut her wild, wild eyes
With kisses four.

And there she lulled me asleep,
And there I dream'd – Ah! woe betide!
The latest dream I ever dream'd
On the cold hill side.

I saw pale kings and princes too,
Pale warriors, death-pale were they all;
They cried – 'La Belle Dame sans Merci
Hath thee in thrall!'

I saw their starved lips in the gloam
With horrid warning gaped wide,
And I awoke and found me here
On the cold hill side.

And this is why I sojourn here
Alone and palely loitering,
Though the sedge is withered from the lake,
And no birds sing.

John Keats 1795–1821

Chapter 2

THE LOVING YEAR

Don't forget the times of the year when love is at its most powerful. Here is our guide to the days that symbolise love and its attendant happiness.

May

I cannot tell you how it was;
But this I know: it came to pass
Upon a bright and breezy day
When May was young, ah pleasant May!

As yet the poppies were not born
Between the blades of tender corn
The last eggs had not hatched as yet,
Nor any bird forgone its mate.

I cannot tell you what it was;
But this I know: it did but pass.
It passed away with sunny May,
With all sweet things it passed away,
And left me old, and cold, and grey.

Christina Rossetti 1830–94

BELTAIN (MAY DAY)

~

Beltain is the greatest fertility festival of the year! Represented by the union of Cernunnos (the Lord of Nature) with the Earth Goddess, it is a day for feasting, fun and romance.

Maypoles are still set up in many places: these represent masculine energy, and the traditional dance around them symbolizes the irresistible energy of Life itself.

Women, both young and old, should make a point of going out just before dawn to wash their faces in morning dew to make themselves beautiful (in spirit if not in body!) – if it can be gathered from under an oak or hawthorn tree, so much the better:

> "The lass who at the break of day
> Goes abroad on the first of May
> To wash in dew from the hawthorn tree
> Will ever after lovely be."

Speak the name of the person whose affection you wish to attract while doing so, saying;

"[name] – my wish upon this special day is that my lover you may be."

An old custom also says that if you wash your feet in dew from the marigold flower, you will be able to understand the language of birds – and perhaps give truth to the saying "a little bird told me . . ."

Those wishing to attract a lover should wear oak or hawthorn leaves, primroses, or a daisy chain. Women wishing to become pregnant should touch an apple or cherry tree – or, even better, join in the dance around a Maypole!

Sonnet 18

~

Shall I compare thee to a summer's day?
Thou art more lovely and more temperate:
Rough winds do shake the darling buds of
    May,
And summer's lease hath all too short a
    date:
Sometime too hot the eye of heaven shines,
And often is his gold complexion dimm'd,
And every fair from fair sometime declines,
By chance, or nature's changing course
    untrimm'd:
But thy eternal summer shall not fade,
Nor lose possession of that fair thou owest,
Nor shall death brag thou wandrest in his
    shade,
When in eternal lines to time thou growest,
So long as men can breathe, or eyes can see
So long lives this, and this gives life to thee.
    William Shakespeare 1564–1616

MIDSUMMER SOLSTICE

❧

Midsummer Eve is the best time in the year for love magic. Ideally, you should stay up all night to watch the sunrise — preferably in the company of your beloved: doing so should ensure that your love will stay fresh and true for another year! However, if you do fall asleep, try to remember your dreams: it is said that midsummer dreams will always come true (no mention is made of nightmares, so we can safely assume that they will not . . .)

If you don't have a partner, go out before dawn to a hill or high place from which you can watch the sunrise. Take with you a piece of rose quartz and/or malachite (if you have any emerald or peridot jewelry, make a point of wearing it), a small bottle of mead or white wine, and two red roses, cowslip, yarrow, clover or daisies — if possible, pick the flowers on your way. Stand facing the rising sun, hold the stones and flowers in front of you, and say:

"I greet you [Sol/Ra/Apollo/Lugh — use your preferred name for the sun] on this most special morning. May love fill my life as your light fills the world."

Pour a few drops of the mead or wine onto the ground, drink a little yourself, and on your return eat a meal of wholegrain bread and fresh oranges to complete the spell!

Vitae Summa Brevis

~

They are not long, the weeping and the
    laughter,
Love and desire and hate:
I think they have no portion in us after
We pass the gate.

They are not long, the days of wine and
    roses:
Out of a misty dream
Our path emerges for a while, then closes
Within a dream.

Ernest Dowson   1867–1900

Friendship After Love

After the fierce midsummer all ablaze
Has burned itself to ashes, and expires
In the intensity of its own fires,
There come the mellow, mild, St Martin
    days
Crowned with the calm of peace, but sad
    with haze.
So after Love has led us, till he tires
Of his own throes, and torments, and
    desires,
Comes large-eyed friendship: with a restful
    gaze,
He beckons us to follow, and across
Cool verdant vales we wander free from
    care.
Is it a touch of frost lies in the air?
Why are we haunted with a sense of loss?
We do not wish the pain back, or the heat;
And yet, and yet, these days are incomplete.

Ella Wheeler Wilcox 1850–1919

LUGHNASADH

~

Lughnasadh (pronounced LOO nah sah – August 1) is the festival of the first fruits of the year's harvest. This is an ideal time for those who have been partners for some time (years rather than months!) to reaffirm their love for each other, and weave a little magic to ensure that love continues for years to come.

Wearing the appropriate colors (red for the male, green for the female) and flowers (oak leaves or heather for the male, poppies or sunflower for the female), you should both go into the countryside: if you can get access to a wheatfield, so much the better, but anywhere food is grown is fine – a farm, vineyard, orchard, even your own vegetable patch: whatever is most convenient. Take along a small symbolic gift for each other. If it should be raining, take a red, green or rainbow-colored umbrella with you!

Find a secluded spot in your chosen location, kneel on the ground facing each other (if it's muddy, stand facing each other instead), exchange gifts, hold hands, and say to each other:

"I thank you for your trust, your friendship and

your affection. In this place, on the good Earth, I celebrate our love: may it grow and flourish, bright and nourishing as the harvest."

Finish with a hearty hug and a kiss (if the weather is fine and the place private enough, you could take this further . . .).

Brussels and Oxford

~

How first we met do you still remember?
Do you still remember our last adieu?
You were all to me, that sweet September:
Oh, what, I wonder, was I to you?

But I will not ask. I will leave in haze
My thoughts of you, and your thoughts of
   me;
And will rest content that those sweet fleet
   days
Are still my tenderest memory.

I often dream how we went together
Mid glimmering leaves and glittering lights,
And watched the twilight Belgian weather
Dying into the starriest nights;

And over our heads the throbbing million
Of bright fires beat, like my heart, on high;
And the music clashed from the lit pavilion,
And we were together, you and I.

But a hollow memory now suffices
For what, last summer, was real and true;
Since here I am by the misty Isis,
And under the fogs of London you.

But what if you, like a swift magician,
Were to change the failing, flowerless year –
Were to make that true that is now a vision
And to bring back summer and Brussels
   here?

For Fanny, I know, that if you come hither
You will bring with you the time of flowers,
And a breath of the tender Belgian weather,
To Oxford's grey autumnal towers.

And in frost and fog though the late year
   dies,
Yet the hours again will be warm and fair,
If they meet once more in your dark, deep
   eyes,
And are meshed again in your golden hair.

William Hurrell Mallock 1849–1923

HARVEST

The Autumn Equinox celebrates the fullness of the year's harvest. It's a special time for older lovers and partners, especially if they have children. To keep the flame of family love alive, organize a special meal.

Decorate the table with acorns, pinecones, corn dollies or kirn babies, poppies and nuts (especially hazel, which is reputed to endow the eater with wisdom); light straw-colored or dark green candles; and ensure the meal includes bread, a lot of different root vegetables, and blackberries. When all the family have assembled, hold hands around the table and say:

"[Demeter/Gaia/Great Mother — use any deity name that seems most suitable to you] we give you thanks for all the good things you have given us: the food we eat, the life we enjoy, the love we share. Teach us to treat you with respect and love throughout the coming year. We ask your blessing on us all."

Save a little of the food and drink (no more than will fit on a small saucer) and at the end of the meal, bury it in the ground — in your yard if you have one, or in a favorite spot out of doors. This symbolic gift acts as a thanksgiving offering to the nurturing Earth, affirming your appreciation for her bounty.

from **Ruth**

~

Round her eyes her tresses fell,
Which were blackest none could tell,
But long lashes veiled a light,
That had else been all too bright.

And her hat, with shady brim,
Made her tressy forehead dim;
Thus she stood amid the stooks,
Praising God with sweetest looks: –

Sure, I said, heaven did not mean,
Where I reap thou shouldst but glean,
Lay thy sheaf adown and come,
Share my harvest and my home.

Thomas Hood 1799–1845

An Evil Spirit

~

An evil spirit, your beauty haunts me still,
Wherewith (alas) I have been long possess'd,
Which ceaseth not to tempt me to each ill,
Nor gives me once, but one poor minute's
    rest:
In me it speaks, whether I sleep or wake,
And when by means, to drive it out I try,
With greater torments then it me doth take,
And tortures me in most extremity;
Before my face, it lays down my despairs,
And hastes me on unto a sudden death;
Now tempting me, to drown myself in tears,
And then in sighing, to give up my breath;
Thus am I still provok'd to every evil,
By this good wicked spirit, sweet angel
    devil.

Michael Drayton   1563–1631

SAMHAIN

Samhain (pronounced "SAH wen": the night of October 31/November 1) is the ancient Celtic New Year. It marks the start of the Dark Year: at this time the barriers between the human and supernatural worlds grow thin, allowing spirits to pass between the two. It's considered very unlucky to refuse hospitality to strangers, in case they are actually visitors from the otherworld, or the spirits of ancestors come back to check that all is well — for the sake of your personal safety, it's perfectly all right to be hospitable outside your home rather than inviting strangers in! Samhain is the ideal time of year for divination and making wishes . . .

Samhain is known as the Feast of Apples, and any spells you perform at this time of year should involve this magical fruit. At midnight, sit before a mirror with a lighted candle at each side, and brush your hair while eating an apple: the face of your future partner may appear reflected in the glass, looking over your shoulder. Alternatively, hold an apple and stand in front of the mirror; make a wish, then eat the apple —

this should ensure it comes true. (Rather more messily, you could also try taking the seeds from an apple, giving each the name of a potential lover, and sticking them onto your cheeks. The last one to fall off is the most suitable choice for you!)

Stanzas

Oh, come to me in dreams, my love!
I will not ask a dearer bliss;
Come with the starry beams, my love,
And press mine eyelids with thy kiss.

'Twas thus, as ancient fables tell,
Love visited a Grecian maid,
Till she disturbed the sacred spell,
And woke to find her hopes betrayed.

But gentle sleep shall veil my sight,
And Psyche's lamp shall darkling be,
When, in the visions of the night,
Thou dost renew thy vows to me.

Then come to me in dreams, my love,
I will not ask a dearer bliss;
Come with the starry beams, my love,
And press mine eyelids with thy kiss.

Mary Wollstonecraft Shelley 1797–1851

And On My Eyes Dark Sleep By Night

~

Come, dark-eyed Sleep, thou child of
    Night,
Give me thy dreams, thy lies;
Lead through the horny portal white
The pleasure day denies.

O bring the kiss I could not take
From lips that would not give;
Bring me the heart I could not break,
The bliss for which I live.

I care not if I slumber blest
By fond delusion; nay,
Put me on Phaon's lips to rest,
And cheat the cruel day!

Michael Field 1846–1914

YULE

~

The Midwinter Solstice. Yule celebrates the rebirth of the sun – from this day the nights get shorter and the days longer.

Yule is a very special time, full of hope for the year to come. Gifts are exchanged, parties enjoyed, and most of us indulge in rich food, drink and festivities. The atmosphere of abundant goodwill and fellowship at this time of year makes it ideal for approaching the person you've had your eye on and inviting them out, to a party, movie, or just for a walk on a crisp and starry night . . .

Try cutting an apple in half vertically, and count the seeds in each half. If there is an equal number, a romance is forecast for the very near future: however, if one of the seeds has been cut, the relationship will have stormy patches.

Holly and mistletoe are traditional Yuletide plants: the red berries of the holly represent the blood of the Earth Goddess, while the white berries of the mistletoe symbolize the seed of the Sun God (kissing under the mistletoe was originally a fertility charm!)

Holly is a luck-bringer, and mistletoe can act as a charm to ensure your love remains ever-true: kiss your lover under a sprig while repeating, mentally,

"[name], be ever mine."

It would be wise, however, to be certain you wish to spend your life with him or her before trying this spell!

To My Excellent Lucasia

~

I did not live until this time
Crown'd my felicity,
When I could say without a crime,
I am not thine, but Thee.

This carcass breath'd, and walkt, and
    slept,
So that the World Believ'd
There was a soul the motions kept;
But they were all deceiv'd.

For as a watch by art is wound
To motion, such was mine:
But never had Orinda found
A soul till she found thine;

Which now inspires, cures, and supplies,
And guides my darkened breast:
For thou art all that I can prize,
My joy, my Life, my Rest.

No bridegroom's nor crown-conqueror's
   mirth
To mine compared can be:
They have but pieces of the earth,
I've all the World in thee.

Then let our flames still light and shine,
And no false fear control,
As innocent as our design,
Immortal as our soul.

                  Katherine Philips   1632–64

Second Thoughts

I thought of leaving her for a day
In town, it was such iron winter
At Durdans, the garden frosty clay,
The woods as dry as any splinter,
The sky congested. I would break
From the deep, lethargic country air
To the shining lamps, to the clash of the
    play,
And to-morrow, wake
Beside her, a thousand things to say.
I planned – O more – I had almost
    started; –
I lifted her face in my hands to kiss, –
A face in a border of fox's fur,
For the bitter black wind had stricken her,
And she wore it – her soft hair straying out
Where it buttoned against the gray, leather
    snout;
In an instant we should have parted;
But at sight of the delicate world within

That fox-fur collar, from brow to chin,
At sight of those wonderful eyes from the
    mine,
Coal pupils, an iris of glittering spa,
And the wild, ironic, defiant shine
As of a creature behind a bar
One has captured, and, when three lives are
    past,
May hope to reach the heart of at last,
All that, and the love at her lips, combined
To shew me what folly it were to miss
A face with such thousand things to say,
And beside these, such thousand more to
    spare,
For the shining lamps, for the clash of the
    play –
O madness; not for a single day
Could I leave her! I stayed behind.
                    Michael Field 1846–1914

IMBOLC

~

Imbolc (February 1) is often the very coldest time of the year, and Imbolc celebrates the White Lady, the earth slowly awakening into spring. Snowdrops, those lovely little flowers that symbolize "Hope," are just about the only things in flower in colder northern climes, and so have come to represent the optimism of this season.

Imbolc is a good time to practice a little candle-magic. Take a white candle for each of your potential lovers and lightly carve each of their names into the wax — it's best to use quite small candles for this, since ideally you will watch over them until they have all burned out. Depending on the number of candles, position them in a line or a circle, with one pink or blue candle in the middle (or use silver or gold; this candle represents you, and can be in your favorite color if you prefer). You will need to decide, in advance, what sign you wish to reveal your ideal choice: it could be the first candle to burn down or go out, or the last candle to do the same.

When you have decided, light all of the candles,

and sit waiting for your chosen sign to occur. (If you already have a secret preference, you could always try to extinguish, or make to burn until last, the candle for that person. Who knows, you might discover an unrecognized talent for psychokinesis!)

Fire Us With Ice

As Corydon went shiv'ring by,
Sylvia a Ball of Snow let fly,
Which straight a Globe of Fire became,
And put the Shepherd in a Flame;
Cupid now break thy Darts and Bow,
Sylvia can all thy Feats out-do,
Fire us with Ice, burn us with Snow.

Mary Monk 1677–1715

Between Your Sheets

~

Between your sheets you soundly sleep
Nor dream of vigils that we lovers keep
While all the night, I waking sigh your
    name,
The tender sound does every nerve inflame,
Imagination shows me all your charms,
The plenteous silken hair and waxen arms,
The well turned neck and snowy rising
    breast
And all the beauties that supinely rest
between your sheets.

Ah Lindamira, could you see my heart,
How fond, how true, how free from fraudful
    art,
The warmest glances poorly do explain
The eager wish, the melting throbbing pain
Which through my very blood and soul I
    feel,
Which you cannot believe nor I reveal,

Which every metaphor must render less
And yet (methinks) which I could well
   express
between your sheets.
   Lady Mary Wortley Montagu   1689–1762

Sonnet

I wish I could remember that first day,
First hour, first moment of your meeting
   me.
If bright or dim the season, it might be
Summer or Winter for aught that I can say:
So unrecorded did it slip away,
So blind was I to see and to foresee,
So dull to mark the budding of my tree
That would not blossom yet for many a
   May.
If only I could recollect it, such
A day of days! I let it come and go
As traceless as a thaw of bygone snow;
It seemed to mean so little, meant so much;
If only now I could recall that touch,
First touch of hand in hand. – Did one but
   know!

Christina Rossetti 1830–94

From the Telephone

~

Out of the dark cup
Your voice broke like a flower.
It trembled, swaying on its taut stem.
The caress in its touch
Made my eyes close.
  Florence Ripley Mastin late 19th century

ST VALENTINE'S DAY

~

February 14. This festival has a close association with the lupercalia of ancient Rome, held on February 15, when the beginning of spring was celebrated with wild and orgiastic festivities! It is sacred to lovers, and the perfect time for love spells . . .

Place bay leaves under your pillow and recite –
"Let this night be good to me,
And I in dreams my true love see."

February 14 in a Leap Year was, traditionally, the time when a woman could propose marriage to her beloved. He didn't have to accept, of course – but if he refused he was supposed to buy her a pure silk gown as consolation . . .

These days, treating your loved one to a special meal, or flowers and chocolates, are more usual offerings. You could try including some of the traditional aphrodisiacs, or foods of love, in the meal: oysters, asparagus, truffles, strawberries, honey, cream-filled or chocolate confections (and worry about the diet the following day . . .).

To cast a special Valentine's day spell, take

strawberries (for promises of delights to come), cherries (for lively romance), hazelnuts (for wise choices) or brazil nuts (for good luck in love): melt chocolate in a bowl over a pan of boiling water and dunk the fruit and nuts one at a time into the chocolate, making an appropriate wish as you do so. Cool the sweets on greaseproof paper, then place them in tissue in a pretty box and give them to your loved one as a gift. (You might like to make a note of how many – and which – of the wishes come true!)

All Thoughts, All Passions

All thoughts, all passions, all delights,
Whatever stirs this mortal frame,
All are but ministers of Love,
And feed his sacred flame.
Samuel Taylor Coleridge   1772–1834

Once We Played

Once we played at love together –
Played it smartly, if you please;
Lightly, as a windblown feather,
Did we stake a heart apiece.

Oh, it was delicious fooling!
In the hottest of the game,
Without thought of future cooling,
All too quickly burned Life's flame.

In this give-and-take of glances,
Kisses sweet as honey dews,
When we played with equal chances,
Did you win, or did I lose?

Mathilde Blind 1841–96

EOSTRE

~

The Vernal (Spring) Equinox is a time of rejoicing that spring, with all its attendant happiness, has arrived. And of course, in Spring "a young man's (and woman's) fancy turns to love . . ."

This is the festival of Eostre, the ancient goddess of spring fertility. Hares and eggs are her symbols, and – weather permitting – this is an excellent time for loving couples to take a walk in the country (or at least the local park!) and enjoy both the general feel-good atmosphere and each other's company. If you can find some violets, so much the better – they symbolize constancy, modesty and faithfulness. Stand by the patch and indulge in a long, lingering kiss, but be careful not to crush any of the flowers!

Try a little egg magic. Take the (clean!) rounded end of an eggshell, place in it a scrap of paper with the name of your beloved written on it. Light a yellow or light green candle and allow the wax to drip onto and over the paper until it is completely sealed in a covering of wax, but don't fill the eggshell: it must be able to float. Take it to the nearest water source and cast it carefully adrift on the water, saying with all your heart:

"[Name], as I set you free, may you choose to stay with me,

Wheresoever you may roam, may I always be your home."

I Will Not Give Thee All My Heart

~

I will not give thee all my heart
For that I need a place apart
To dream my dreams in and I know
Few sheltered ways for dreams to go:
But when I shut the door upon
Some secret wonder – still, withdrawn –
Why does thou love me even more,
And hold me closer than before?

When I of love demand the least,
Thou biddest him to fire and feast:
When I am hungry and would eat,
There is no bread, though crusts were
    sweet.
If I with manna may be fed,
Shall I go all uncomforted?
Nay! Howsoever dear thou art,
I will not give thee all my heart.

   Grace Hazard Conkling late 19th century

To Anthea

Bid me to live, and I will live
Thy Protestant to be;
Or bid me love, and I will give
A loving heart to thee.

A heart as soft, a heart as kind,
A heart as sound and free,
As in the whole world thou canst find,
That heart I'll give to thee.

Bid that heart stay, and it will stay,
To honour thy decree;
Or bid it languish quite away,
And 't shall do so for thee.

Bid me to weep, and I will weep,
While I have eyes to see;
And having none, yet I will keep
A heart to weep for thee.

Bid me despair, and I'll despair,
Under that cypress tree;
Or bid me die, and I will dare
E'en death, to die for thee.

Thou art my life, my love, my heart,
The very eyes of me;
And hast command of every part,
To live and die for thee.

Robert Herrick   1591–1674

Marriage Morning

Light, so low upon earth,
You send a flash to the sun.
Here is the golden close of love,
All my wooing is done.
Oh, the woods and the meadows,
Woods where we hid from the wet,
Stiles where we stay'd to be kind,
Meadows in which we met!

Light, so low in the vale
You flash and lighten afar,
For this is the golden morning of love,
And you are his morning star.
Flash, I am coming, I come,
By meadow and stile and wood,
Oh, lighten into my eyes and heart,
Into my heart and my blood!

Heart, are you great enough
For a love that never tires?

O heart, are you great enough for love?
I have heard of thorns and briers.
Over the thorns and briers,
Over the meadows and stiles,
Over the world to the end of it
Flash for a million miles.

Alfred, Lord Tennyson 1809–92

Sonnet 116

~

Let me not to the marriage of true minds
Admit impediments. Love is not love
Which alters when it alteration finds,
Or bends with the remover to remove:
O, no, it is an ever-fixed mark,
That looks on tempests and is never
    shaken;
It is the star to every wandering bark,
Whose worth's unknown, although his
    height be taken.
Love's not Time's fool, though rosy lips
    and cheeks
Within his bending sickle's compass
    come;
Love alters not with his brief hours and
    weeks,
But bears it out even to the edge of doom.
If this be error and upon me proved,
I never writ, nor no man ever loved.

        William Shakespeare 1564–1616

Delight in Disorder

~

A sweet disorder in the dresse
Kindles in cloathes a wantonnesse:
A Lawne about the shoulders thrown
Into a fine distraction: —
An erring Lace, which here and there
Enthralls the Crimson Stomacher: —
A Cuffe neglectfull, and thereby
Ribbands to flow confusedly: —
A winning wave (deserving Note)
In the tempestuous petticote: —
A carelesse shoe-string, in whose tye
I see a wilde civility: —
Doe more bewitch me, than when Art
Is too precise in every part.

Robert Herrick 1591–1674

Chapter 3

✣

DIVINATION

Most of us would like to know what the future has in store for us, both so that we know what to expect and so that we can prepare for misfortune — hence the vast number of forms of divination available to anyone who cares to search. In the following pages are some of the ways that lovers through the ages have tried to divine the course of their loves. Some are quick and easy, some require a little more effort, but all can be tried by anyone wishing for a glimpse into the future. But be warned — there is no guarantee that any of them can accurately foretell what is to come!

How Long Shall I Pine?

~

How long shall I pine for love?
How long shall I muse in vain?
How long like the turtle-dove
Shall I heavenly thus complain?
Shall the sails of my love stand still?
Shall the grists of my hopes be
    unground?
Oh fie, oh fie, oh fie,
Let the mill, let the mill go round.

John Fletcher 1579–1625

Enflam'd with Love

~

Enflam'd with love and led by blind desires,
The man persues, the blushful maid retires.
He hopes for pleasures, but she fears the
    pain,
His love but ignorance is, her feares more
    vain.
When e're he tast's those joys so pris'd
    before
He'll love no longer and she'll feare no
    more.

Charles Sackville, Earl of Dorset
1638–1706

FIRE

～

Touch a corner of a love-letter to a flame (or use the envelope if the letter is too precious to burn). If the flame is strong and bright, the relationship, and your lover, is staunch and true. However, if it is meager, or goes out, or won't light at all, then beware — regardless of the words, the relationship is all but dead.

A variation of this is to write the name of your lover on a piece of paper and hold it to the flame of a white candle. Again, a reluctant flame indicates a dying relationship, and a strong flame a strong love — but if the paper flares and burns to ash almost immediately, beware: too hot a passion dies quickly!

Take a red (if you're female) or green (if you're male) candle and push a pin into it, about halfway down. Light the candle and time how long it takes to burn down far enough for the pin to fall. The longer the time, the stronger the love, and the longer it will last. If the pin doesn't fall from the candle, but slowly slides down the side, you are likely to remain together for the rest of your lives . . .

Song

Nothing ades to Loves fond fire
More than scorn and cold disdain
I to cherish your desire
Kindness used but twas in vain
You insulted on your slave
To be mine you soon refused
Hope not then the power to have
Which ingloriously you used
Think not Thersis I will ere
By my love my empire loose
You grow constant through dispare
Kindness you would soon abuse
Though you still possess my heart
Scorn and rigor I must fain
There remains no other art
Your love fond fugitive to gain.

Elizabeth Wilmot d. 1681

from A Fragment

For when in Floods of Love we're
    drench'd,
The Flames are by enjoyment quench'd:
But thus, let's thus together lie,
And kiss out long Eternity:
Here we dread no conscious spies,
No blushes stain our guiltless Joys:
Here no Faintness dulls Desires,
And Pleasure never flags, nor tires:
This has pleas'd, and pleases now,
And for Ages will do so:
Enjoyment here is never down,
But fresh, and always but begun.

                Petronius   1st century AD

AIR

〜

Sneezes have been used in a counting rhyme to foretell the romantic prospects for the next few days ...

> "One sneeze – a kiss
> Two – a wish come true
> Three – a love letter
> Four – something even better!"

Presumably sneezing more than four times means you have a cold, and are out of the romantic running until it's cleared up!

There is an older variant of the rhyme:

"Sneeze on a Monday, sneeze for danger;
Sneeze on a Tuesday, kiss a stranger;
Sneeze on a Wednesday, expect a letter;
Sneeze on a Thursday for something better;
Sneeze on a Friday, sneeze for sorrow;
Sneeze on a Saturday, see your sweetheart
tomorrow;
Sneeze on a Sunday, your safety
seek –
Bad luck will dog you the whole of the week."

If you are single and looking for a partner, try bird watching on St Valentine's day. A superstition states that the bird you see first on February 14 foretells the status and occupation of your future mate:

Blackbird – an older man or woman, in business or religion.

Magpie or Jay – a charming rogue who'll steal your heart away – and leave you lonely.

Robin – a cheerful person, in one of the caring professions.

Pigeon or Dove – a good, honest, loving person, one who works with their hands or for the good of the planet.

Hen or Duck – a homemaker, brusque, efficient and kindly.

Tit or Finch – a younger person, possibly flighty, difficult to pin down but a lot of fun!

Owl – an older person, in the legal or academic professions.

Sparrow or Starling – a homely person of little ambition but much endurance.

Swan – a dignified person, one who travels a lot.

Hawk or Eagle – a noble, high-principled person, possibly connected with the armed forces.

Crow or Rook – a strict, careful man or woman, in banking, insurance or other financial business.

Exotic bird (macaw, cockatoo etc.) – an extravagant person, an actor or artist.

from Aire and Angels

Twice or thrice had I lov'd thee,
Before I knew thy face or name;
So in a voice, so in a shapelesse flame,
Angels affect us oft, and worship'd be;
Still when, to where thou wert, I came,
Some lovely glorious nothing I did see.
But since my soule, whose child love is,
Takes limmes of flesh, and else could
    nothing doe,
More subtile than the parent is,
Love must not be, but take a body too,
And therefore what thou wert, and who,
I bid Love aske, and now
That it assume thy body, I allow,
And fixe it selfe in thy lip, eye, and brow.

John Donne 1572–1631

from Silent Is the House

~

Come, the wind may never again
Blow as now it blows for us;
And the stars may never again shine as
    now they shine;
Long before October returns,
Seas of blood will have parted us;
And you must crush the love in your
    heart, and I the love in mine!

                Emily Brontë 1818–48

A Song

Absent from thee, I languish still;
Then ask me not, when I return?
The straying fool 'twill plainly kill
To wish all day, all night to mourn.

Dear! from thine arms then let me fly,
That my fantastic mind may prove
The torments it deserves to try
That tears my fixed heart from my love.

When, wearied with a world of woe,
To thy safe bosom I retire
Where love and peace and truth does flow,
May I contented there expire,

Lest, once more wandering from that
    heaven,
I fall on some base heart unblest,
Faithless to thee, false, unforgiven,
And lose my everlasting rest.

John Wilmot, Earl of Rochester 1647–80

WATER

~

Next time you have a cup of tea or coffee, look carefully at the surface. If there are bubbles floating, there is a kiss coming your way in the very near future! Inviting someone to join you in a cappuccino could, therefore, be either the prelude to a romantic interlude, or a dangerous occupation . . .

Putting milk or cream in the tea or coffee before you add the sugar or honey is an omen of lost love — although, of course, if you don't take a sweetener you can ignore this one. Furthermore, if two spoons are accidentally placed on one saucer, it's a sign of a wedding in the near future!

from Love at Large

Whene'er I come where ladies are,
How sad soever I was before,
Though like a ship frost-bound and far
Withheld in ice from the ocean's roar,
Third-wintered in that dreadful dock,
With stiffened cordage, sails decayed,
And crew that care for calm and shock
Alike, too dull to be dismayed,
Yet, if I come where ladies are,
How sad soever I was before,
Then is my sadness banished far,
And I am like that ship no more.

Coventry Patmore   1823–96

A Farewell

'And if I did, what then?
Are you aggrieved therefore?
The sea hath fish for every man,
And what would you have more?'

Thus did my mistress once
Amaze my mind with doubt;
And popped a question for the nonce,
To beat my brains about.

Whereto I thus replied:
'Each fisherman can wish,
That all the seas at every tide
Were his alone to fish.

'And so did I, in vain,
But since it may not be,
Let such fish there as find the gain,
And leave the loss for me.

'And with such luck and loss
I will content myself,
Till tides of turning time may toss
Such fishers on the shelf.

'And when they stick on sands,
That every man may see,
Then will I laugh and clap my hands,
As they do now at me.'

George Gascoigne 1525–77

EARTH

~

To find out if your future mate will be dark or fair-haired, take a table knife with a white handle and spin it in a circle on a table. If it stops with the blade towards you, your lover will be dark-haired: if with the haft, expect a blond! (If it falls off the table it warns of the abrupt end to the romance.)

It's a very good omen if your hand shakes while you write a love letter – and if you should blot the letter (not a common occurrence unless you write with a pen using real ink) even better: it presages happiness in the very near future.

For an unusual divination, scratch the names of possible lovers on pieces of cheese and leave them somewhere cool. The first piece that becomes moldy is the ideal lover!

Alternatively, you can leave the cheese pieces in the cage of a mouse or rat. The first piece that is eaten then represents the person on whom you should concentrate your affections.

I Showed Her Heights

~

I showed her Heights she never saw –
'Wouldst Climb' I said?
She said – 'Not so' –
'With me –' I said – With me?
I showed her Secrets – Morning's Nest –
The Rope the Nights were put across –
And now – 'Would'st have me for a
   Guest?'
She could not find her Yes –
And then, I brake my life – And Lo,
A Light, for her, did solemn glow,
The larger, as her face withdrew –
And could she, further, 'No'?

Emily Dickinson 1830–86

Remember

~

Remember me when I am gone away,
Gone far away into the silent land;
When you can no more hold me by the
　　hand,
Nor I half turn to go yet turning stay.
Remember me when no more day by day
You tell me of our future that you
　　planned:
Only remember me; you understand
It will be late to counsel then or pray.
Yet if you should forget me for a while
And afterwards remember, do not grieve:
For if the darkness and corruption leave
A vestige of the thoughts that once I had,
Better by far you should forget and smile
Than that you should remember and be
　　sad.

Christina Rossetti 1830–94

Chapter 4

~≈·&·≈~

ANIMAL MAGIC

Certain birds and animals have a reputation for possessing qualities and characteristics which may prove helpful in your romantic life — either because they provide something that you feel is lacking, or simply as a symbol of your hopes and desires.

Images of these creatures — talismans — can be worn as jewelry (rings, pendants or earrings, for example), as carved figurines in your home or office, as tattoos (but be absolutely certain you're happy with the totem before you do anything so permanent) or you can even dress and make-up to symbolize the creature itself — if you have the nerve to do so!

Modern fabrics can create the effect of iridescent feathers or scales, and there are plenty of realistic-looking fake furs available (we wouldn't endorse the use of real fur), while modern cosmetics provide plenty of vibrant color for face, body and hair. You are only limited by your imagination . . .

SWAN

~

The swan symbolizes the epitome of romantic love. Beautiful, graceful and lordly, the sight of swans on a tranquil stretch of river is enough to stir even the most jaded soul.

Swans are faithful birds, and make tender, caring parents. They are also fiercely protective of their mates and brood. Their reputation of mating for life has made them the ideal totem for the couple who wish to keep their partnership strong and sure.

Swans "dance" during their courtship, creating living "heart" shapes with their heads and necks as they mirror each other's movements. To bring a little swan-magic into your life, try taking dance classes (old time or ballroom, though, not line dancing or disco!)

Love's Philosophy

~

The fountains mingle with the river
And the rivers with the ocean,
The winds of heaven mix for ever
With a sweet emotion;
Nothing in the world is single,
All things by a law divine
In one another's being mingle –
Why not I with thine?

See the mountains kiss high heaven
And the waves clasp one another;
No sister-flower would be forgiven
If it disdain'd its brother:

And the sunlight clasps the earth,
And the moonbeams kiss the sea –
What are all these kissings worth,
If thou kiss not me?

Percy Bysshe Shelley 1792–1822

DOVE

~

The dove is special to Aphrodite, and is representative of the sweetness of young love (young in the sense of new and fresh rather than just for young people). Their soft, cooing call is one of the delights of summer, and has led to the phrase "billing and cooing."

Keep a statuette of a pair of doves near the entrance to your home, to help safeguard your domestic happiness. But remember that dove-magic is gentle and homely, so don't keep images — or the birds themselves — if you want excitement in your life.

To help reconcile yourself to the loss of a lover, buy a dove and set it free.

Sonnet 113

Since I left you, mine eye is in my mind,
And that which governs me to go about
Doth part his function and is partly blind,
Seems seeing, but effectually is out;
For it no form delivers to the heart
Of bird, of flower, or shape, which it doth
    latch:
Of his quick objects hath the mind no part.
Nor his own vision holds what it doth catch;
For if it see the rudest or gentlest sight,
The most sweet favour or deformed'st
    creature,
The mountain or the sea, the day or night,
The crow or dove, it shapes them to your
    feature:
Incapable of more, replete with you,
My most true mind thus maketh mine
    untrue.

William Shakespeare 1564–1616

PEACOCK

Included here more as a warning! The peacock is one of the most impressive and beautiful of all birds, but it also has the reputation of being vain, silly and pretentious. Its purpose is purely decorative, and it has a loud and ugly voice.

If you find yourself attracted to the human version of the peacock, as many people do, you may find you have to fight for their attention. However, if you wish to bring a little glamor into your own life, try owning a peacock feather fan or a luxurious, peacock-colored article of clothing. Do try not to imitate either the bird or its human counterpart, though, or you could end up looking foolish!

A Birthday

~

My heart is like a singing bird
Whose nest is in a watered shoot;
My heart is like a rainbow shell
That paddles in a halcyon sea;
My heart is gladder than all these
Because my love is come to me.

Raise me a dais of silk and down;
Hang it with vair and purple dyes;
Carve it in doves and pomegranates
And peacocks with a hundred eyes;
Work it in gold and silver grapes,
In leaves and silver fleurs-de-lys;
Because the birthday of my life
Is come, my love is come to me.

Christina Rossetti 1830–94

DEER

Deer are often seen as symbolic of the softer, gentler side of nature. An attractive epithet for a loving, tender woman is "doe-eyed" (the aggressive behavior of the stags in the rutting season tends to be largely ignored in such idealistic contemplation!) In Chinese lore, the deer symbolizes immortality, and may be viewed as representing an undying relationship.

In considering deer-magic, it is important to be very sure that the relationship is one you wish to continue, since once invoked, it is difficult to cancel — and you may find yourself trapped in an unhappy situation with no way out.

To My Heavenly Charmer

My poor expecting Heart beats for thy
    Breast,
In ev'ry pulse, and will not let me rest;
A thousand dear Desires are waking there,
Whose softness will not a Description bear,
Oh! let me pour them to thy lovely eyes,
And catch their tender meanings as they
    rise.
My ev'ry Feature with my Passion glows
In ev'ry thought and look it overflows.
Too noble and too strong for all Disguise,
It rushes from my love-discov'ring Eyes.
Nor Rules nor Reason can my Love
    restrain;
Its godlike Tide runs high in ev'ry Vein.
To the whole World my Tenderness be
    known,
What is the World to her, who lives for thee
    alone.

Martha Sansom 1690–1736

LION

~

The lion has the reputation of being the king of the beasts, but actually this epithet is somewhat misplaced. Lions may *look* regal, but it is the lioness that hunts and provides the food: the lion is something of a parasite, mostly dependent on the female for his existence. As a totem, the lioness is far more appropriate, especially for the single woman looking for an exciting, but not necessarily permanent, relationship. That being said, a full, mane-like hairstyle may prove very effective as a charm to generate lion-magic.

If possible wear jewelry resembling claws and teeth (but preferably not the real thing), and sleek tawny-colored clothing. Practice a direct, business-like approach to people, and accept admiration as your due!

Renouncement

I must not think of thee; and, tired yet
    strong,
I shun the love that lurks in all delight –
The love of thee – and in the blue
    heaven's height,
And in the dearest passage of a song.
O just beyond the fairest thoughts that
    throng
This breast, the thought of thee waits,
    hidden yet bright;
But it must never, never come in sight;
I must stop short of thee the whole day
    long.

But when sleep comes to close each
    difficult day,
When night gives pause to the long
    watch I keep,
And all my bonds I needs must loose
    apart,

Must doff my will as raiment laid
    away, –
With the first dream that comes with the
    first sleep
I run, I run, I am gathered to thy heart.
             Alice Meynell 1847–1922

TIGER

~

"Tyger! Tyger! Burning bright
In the forests of the night,
What immortal hand or eye
Could frame thy fearful symmetry?"

William Blake

If the lion is the king of the African plains, the tiger is his equal in the Asian forests. Noble, sensitive and courageous, the tiger is the perfect totem for the person (male or female) who – through choice or happenstance – lives a solitary life but still wants a romantic attachment. Tiger's eye (the beautiful semi-precious stone) set in gold makes perfect jewelry for such a person. Wearing clothes with subtle stripes and shading may also help to generate tiger-magic.

A Moment

The clouds had made a crimson crown
Above the mountains high.
The stormy sun was going down
In a stormy sky.

Why did you let your eyes so rest on me,
And hold your breath between?
In all the ages this can never be
As if it had not been.
Mary Elizabeth Coleridge 1861–1907

WOLF

~

The wolf represents the strong protector: it symbolizes wildness, the natural world and inner strength. Traditionally, it is also seen as a helpful guide, especially for the lost traveler. Although usually viewed as a dangerous predator, in the sphere of love-magic the wolf can act as a totem of protection in a tense situation or relationship.

Due in part to the wolf's significance in Native American lore, in the absence of more obvious wolf imagery Amerindian silver and turquoise jewelry may be worn talismanically to help bring the animal's influence into your life.

Love's Philosophy

The fountains mingle with the river
And the rivers with the ocean,
The winds of heaven mix for ever
With a sweet emotion;
Nothing in the world is single,
All things by a law divine
In one another's being mingle –
Why not I with thine?

See the mountains kiss high heaven
And the waves clasp one another;
No sister-flower would be forgiven
If it disdain'd its brother:
And the sunlight clasps the earth,
And the moonbeams kiss the sea –
What are all these kissings worth,
If thou kiss not me?

Percy Bysshe Shelley 1792–1822

FOX

~

The fox is a shrewd and clever animal, with a reputation for being able to extricate itself from tricky situations — the ideal symbol for those who are forever finding themselves tangled up in complicated love lives!

It's usually not too difficult to find representations of the fox, either as jewelry, on clothing, or even key-rings: you might find it useful to use one of these latter for your car keys (to help you make a quick escape from awkward situations . . .) In such circumstances, you might also find it helpful to address a quick petition to the spirit of the fox, perhaps asking that you not be found out!

On Her Loving Two Equally

How strongly does my passion flow,
Divided equally 'twixt two?
Damon had ne'er subdued my heart,
Had not Alexis took his part
Nor could Alexis powerful prove
Without my Damon's aid, to gain my love.

When my Alexis present is,
Then I for Damon sigh and mourn;
But when Alexis I do miss,
Damon gains nothing but my scorn
But if it chance they both are by
For both alike I languish, sigh and die.

Cure then, thou mighty winged god
This restless fever in my blood;
One golden-pointed dart take back
But which, O Cupid, wilt thou take?
If Damon's, all my hopes are crossed;
Or that of my Alexis, I am lost.

Aphra Behn 1640–89

DOG

~

The domestic dog comes in an enormous range of sizes, shapes and colors, even more so than the cat. As with the cat, the breed you choose can represent either the sort of person you are or how you would like to be seen, but whereas another person will only get to know your cat once they've been welcomed into your home, a dog is admired in the outside world, and is often a more obvious symbol of your personality. The stylish Afghan, for example, presents a completely different image than does a pugnacious Jack Russell, a sporty Retriever, or a snooty Pekinese: and you can use these visual clues not only to express your own personality, but also to give you an insight into the nature of potential lovers!

Dogs are far less independent animals than cats, and require a lot more care and company. They are also blindly affectionate, and will repay many-fold love you give them, unconditionally and without asking for much more than food, walks and the occasional hug in return. If you truly find it difficult to find your ideal human love, but (like most of us) need a loving companion, a dog may prove to be, not, of course, a substitute, but nevertheless a cherished friend.

Dear, Why Make You More of a Dog?

~

Dear, why make you more of a dog than me?
If he do love, I burn, I burn in love:
If he wait well, I never thence would move:
If he be fair, yet but a dog can be.
Little he is, so little worth is he;
He barks, my songs thine own voice oft doth
    prove:
Bidd'n, perhaps he fetcheth thee a glove,
But I unbid, fetch even my soul to thee.
Yet while I languish, him that bosom clips,
That lap doth lap, nay lets, in spite of spite,
This sour-breath'd mate taste of those
    sugar'd lips.
Alas, if you grant only such delight
To witless things, the Love I hope (since wit
Becomes a clog) will soon ease me of it.

Sir Philip Sidney 1554–86

DOMESTIC CATS

~

The household cat comes in a vast array of pattern, colors and temperaments! Simply owning one of these lovely felines adds cat-magic to your life: the breed says a great deal about the sort of person you are (or want to be!). A silver tabby, for example, is a little like a scaled-down tiger, suggesting hints of wildness beneath the surface, while a Siamese implies breeding, refinement and a touch of arrogance. Burmese — in fact most of the longhaired breeds — symbolize luxury and gracious living. Black cats are mysterious, bewitching creatures, and very often the enchantment rubs off on their humans!

And of course, there is always the kitten — playful, impish, mischievous, the sort of small creature that people just can't help loving and wanting to look after . . . Some cats remain kittens all their lives, and are delightfully youthful well into old age.

Obviously, owning a cat (or having it own you, which is more often true) is a big responsibility and not to be undertaken lightly — and there is always the risk that your intended beloved doesn't like cats (in which case perhaps you should consider choosing a different lover!) But cats bring love into your life, and if you feel loved, and relaxed, you will automatically become more attractive to others – and that's where the true magic of the love spell lies!

Sonnet from the Portuguese XIV

~

If thou must love me, let it be for nought
Except for love's sake only. Do not say
'I love her for her smile ... her look ... her
    way
Of speaking gently, – for a trick of thought
That falls in well with mine, and certes
    brought
A sense of pleasant ease on such a day' –
For these things in themselves, Beloved,
    may
be changed, or change for thee, – and love,
    so wrought
May be unwrought so. Neither love me for
Thine own dear pity's wiping my cheeks dry,
Since one might well forget to weep who
    bore
Thy comfort long, and lose thy love thereby.
But love me for love's sake, that evermore
Thou may'st love on through love's eternity.
Elizabeth Barrett Browning 1806–61

Chapter 5

LOVE IN THE STARS

Synastry is the astrological art of matching two individual horoscopes to measure the compatability (or otherwise!) of the people involved. Obviously, to gain a true picture it is necessary to cast the natal charts — but the following pages can give you some idea, in very general terms, how love and romance affect each of the Zodiac Signs. By checking your own Sign and that of your partner, you should be able to gain some idea of what to expect — and how to react!

When I Was Fair and Young
~

When I was fair and young, then favour
    graced me;
Of many was I sought their mistress for to be,
But I did scorn them all, and answered them
    therefore:
'Go! go! go! seek some other where,
    importune me no more!'

How many weeping eyes, I made to pine with
    woe!
How many sighing hearts! I have no skill to
    show.
Yet I the prouder grew, and still this spake
    therefore:
'Go! go! go! seek some other where,
    importune me no more!'

Then spake fair Venus' son that proud
    victorious boy,
Saying: You dainty dame for that you be so
    coy?

I will so pluck your plumes that you shall say
    no more:
'Go! go! go! seek some other where,
    importune me no more!'

As soon as he had said, such change grew in
    my breast,
That neither night nor day, I could take any
    rest.
Then lo! I did repent that I had said before:
'Go! go! go! seek some other where,
    importune me no more.'

Queen Elizabeth I 1533–1603

ARIES IN LOVE

~

Man Forceful, passionate, uncompromising, easily bored! The male Aries has a tendency to place his beloved on a pedestal. To keep him interested, keep him surprised with changes of images, new ideas and novel things to do. If you want to keep him, never let yourself become predictable – and never let him think he owns you.

Woman Dominant, passionate, not always the most faithful of people! The female Aries loves a challenge, but may also see her partner as a contestant in a battle of wills. Play hard to get, treat her to unusual experiences and presents, and make sure you never become boring.

Suggested Gifts A day out at a safari or theme park; a disposable camera.

Charm to Attract an Aries

~

The best day to perform this spell is Thursday, and the best place a hilltop. Dress entirely in red, and wear red jewelry — especially rubies if you own any: the ruby is Aries' birth stone.

Take something made of iron — an iron nail, or, even better, a small piece of meteoric iron — and a single, bright red candle. If possible, light some citrus-scented incense (a joss stick is ideal if you're out of doors). Hold the lit candle and iron in front of you, and focus on the candle flame as you repeat, mentally: "[name], by fire and iron I conjure you to me."

Carry the iron with you at all times!

The Vain Advice

Ah, gaze not on those eyes! forbear
That soft enchanting voice to hear:
Not looks of basilisks give surer death,
Nor Syrens sing with more destructive
    breath.

Fly, if thy freedom thoud'st maintain,
Alas! I feel th'advice is vain!
A heart whose safety but in flight does lie,
Is too far lost to have the power to fly.

Catherine Cockburn 1679–1749

TAURUS IN LOVE

Man Stubborn, conservative, "physical," very down-to-earth and deeply concerned with quality. The male Taurus can also be extremely possessive: he likes to "own" his lovers. Behave like a lady, be faithful, and never interrupt him!

Woman Practical, luxury loving, calm, sensuous. The Taurean female is the archetypal "earth mother" and tower of strength. Defer to her common sense, don't play the field, and make sure any gifts are of good quality.

Suggested Gifts Discreet, classy jewelry; Belgian chocolates; a potted Bay Tree.

Charm to Win your Taurean

The best day to perform the spell is Friday: the best places a wildflower meadow or a rose garden. Wear deep green, and emeralds (or malachite) and a copper bangle to represent Venus, the ruler of the Sign.

The rose is the best talisman, preferably as jewelry (as a necklace, for example, or stylized cufflinks) but a scarf, tie or cravat are also appropriate. Hold the object gently to your throat, close your eyes and imagine the other standing with you, gazing into your eyes. If you can also imagine them saying "I love you," so much the better!

Wear the object next time you meet, but don't expect immediate results — Taurus takes these things slowly and carefully!

from **Hymn to Venus**

~

Her sparkling necklace first he laid aside,
Her bracelets next, and braided hair unty'd;
And now his busy hand her zone unbrac'd,
Which girt her radiant robe around her
    waist;
Her radiant robe at last aside was thrown,
Whose rosy hue with dazzling lustre shone.
The Queen of Love the youth thus
    disarray'd,
And on a chair of gold her vestments laid.
Anchises now (so Jove and Fate ordain'd)
The sweet extreme of ecstasy attain'd.

         Homer   750 BC approx.

GEMINI IN LOVE

~

Man Funny, eloquent, fickle, often lacking in staying power! The male Gemini loves to talk, about anything and everything – don't be upset if he insists on answering the phone in the middle of a canoodling session! Romance should be playful, and may be more successful if you take charge . . .

Woman Chatty, flirtatious, teasing, great fun to be with. The Gemini female is generally fashionable, well informed, and restless. Keep your conversation light and stimulating: don't try to curb her vivacity (or caprice), and allow her her freedom if you want her to stay.

Suggested Gifts Internet access or a domain of their own; a mobile phone; a palmtop computer.

Charm to Entice a Gemini

~

An ongoing spell, this, and one that requires work. The best way to woo and win a Gemini is to show yourself to be a fascinating person. Find out the Gemini's address or phone number — or, more likely, their e-mail address — and every few days send them an interesting or unusual snippet of information, or a joke (nothing smutty, please), or an amusing anecdote or poem. Gemini loves puns, and information for its own sake, and often has an eccentric sense of humor; if you can match their sparkling wit you'll have a head start in the romantic stakes. But remember, to keep them, you'll need to continue in the same vein . . .

The Look

~

Strephon kissed me in the spring,
Robin in the fall,
But Colin only looked at me
And never kissed at all.

Strephon's kiss was lost in jest,
Robin's lost in play,
But the kiss in Colin's eyes
Haunts me night and day.

Sara Teasdale 1884–1933

CANCER IN LOVE

~

Man Home loving, quiet, fiercely protective, deeply affectionate. The Cancer male is usually very tender, and relishes intimacy. Cherish him, buy him intimate little gifts, and bear with his occasional moods — but don't mother him, or you risk his acting like a temperamental adolescent!

Woman Maternal, moody, nostalgic, enigmatic. The Cancer female is a very "womanly" woman, sensitive and easily hurt. Be gentle, sympathetic, and a shoulder to cry on. And don't be surprised if she defends you like a tiger against anyone who slights you!

Suggested Gifts An antique mirror, silver photo-frame, hip flask or rag doll; lockable diary.

Charm to Woo your Cancer Lover

~

Monday is the best day, and the seashore the best place (try an aquarium if the sea is too far away): any time between new and full moon is appropriate. Wear white clothing and silver and moonstone jewelry. Take with you two small matching pieces of wearable silver (preferably rings, but a neckchain or bracelet are also appropriate).

Hold both pieces touching, in your cupped hands, and repeat, mentally:

"[name] as the moon draws the sea, may this silver draw you to me: may the power of the sweeping tide keep you always by my side."

Wear one piece and give the other to your prospective lover as a gift.

Meeting at Night

The grey sea and the long black land;
And the yellow half-moon large and low;
And the startled little waves that leap
In fiery ringlets from their sleep,
As I gain the cove with pushing prow,
And quench its speed in the slushy sand.

Then a mile of warm sea-scented beach;
Three fields to cross till a farm appears;
A tap at the pane, the quick sharp scratch
And blue spurt of a lighted match,
And a voice less loud, thro' its joys and
    fears,
Than the two hearts beating each to each!
Robert Browning 1812–89

LEO IN LOVE

Man Magnanimous, wholehearted, generous, a little overwhelming. The Leo man usually expects to be the center of his own "court" of friends — a position he will share with his lover. Be properly appreciative, but don't be surprised if he outshines you!

Woman Loyal, sophisticated, dignified, often wants to share her happiness with the entire world — which is fine unless you want to keep it a secret! The Leo female expects fidelity and respect. Treat her like a queen, and she'll be gracious and loving in return.

Suggested Gifts Anything gold or gold-colored.

Charm to Capture your Lion

~

Sunday is the best day: the best place is a theater, art gallery or zoo. Wear gold or yellow colored clothing, and gold and diamond (or tiger's eye) jewelry – and take a packet of sunflower seeds with you . . .

Write the name of your hoped-for lover on the seed packet, and hold it tightly while enjoying the play/admiring the artworks/watching the big cats. Later, plant the seeds in a sunny spot and visit them regularly, willing your intended's love to grow as the seedlings shoot towards the sun.

Save the seeds of the tallest sunflower to plant next year, to keep your relationship blooming!

from Doctor Faustus

~

Was this the face that launched a thousand
    ships?
And burnt the topless towers of Ilium?
Sweet Helen, make me immortal with a kiss:
Her lips suck forth my soul, see where it flies:
And all is dross that is not Helena:
I will be Paris, and for love of thee,
Instead of Troy shall Wertenberg be sack'd,
And I will combat with weak Menelaus,
And wear thy colours on my plumed crest:
Yea I will wound Achilles in the heel,
And then return to Helen for a kiss.
O thou art fairer than the evening air,
Clad in the beauty of a thousand stars,
Brighter art thou than flaming Jupiter,
When he appear'd to hapless Semele,
More lovely than the monarch of the sky
In wanton Arethusa's azur'd arms,
And none but thou shalt be my paramour.

Christopher Marlowe 1564–93

VIRGO IN LOVE

Man Discriminating, interested in how you feel, and why; may insist on using manuals rather than trusting his own feelings! The Virgo male is usually self-controlled, and hates emotional scenes. Be natural and loving, encourage him to relax, and try to go for walks as often as possible.

Woman Cool, cautious, intelligent, may be a little suspicious of your motives. The Virgo female is competent and capable, and demands a considerable amount of personal space. Be her friend, respect her talents, and share your ideas over mugs of herbal tea!

Suggested Gifts A personal organizer; an aroma-therapy or shiatsu course.

Charm to Engage a Virgo

Wednesday is the best day, and a library the ideal place, to perform the first part of this spell. Wear very pale yellow clothing and take a small lidded tin and a piece of rock crystal with you. Hold the crystal tightly, imagining the face of your chosen Virgo: if possible, imagine holding a conversation with them, telling them quietly and calmly how you feel.

When you feel you have explained your feelings sufficiently, wrap the crystal in a small piece of cotton and place it in the tin. As soon as you can, bury the closed tin in a private spot – a favorite place in the country or a secluded corner of a garden.

Caelica

~

Love, the delight of all well-thinking minds;
Delight, the fruit of virtue dearly loved;
Virtue, the highest good, that reason finds;
Reason, the fire wherein men's thoughts be
    proved;
Are from the world by Nature's power bereft,
And in one creature, for her glory, left.

Beauty, her cover is, the eyes' true pleasure;
In honour's fame she lives, the ears' sweet
    music;
Excess of wonder grows from her true
    measure;
Her worth is passion's wound, and passion's
    physic;
From her true heart, clear springs of wisdom
    flow,
Which imaged in her words and deeds, men
    know.

Time fain would stay, that she might never
    leave her,
Place doth rejoice, that she must needs
    contain her,
Death craves of Heaven, that she may not
    bereave her,
The Heavens know their own, and do
    maintain her;
Delight, love, reason, virtue, let it be,
To set all women light, but only she.

Fulke Greville, Lord Brooke 1554–1628

LIBRA IN LOVE

Man Gentle, eager to please, sometimes shy. The Libra male can be a perfectionist: his idea of romance is often a courtly, platonic affair. Engage him in discussion and debate rather than chat, and take an interest in his hobbies.

Woman Quiet, competent, intellectually inclined yet deeply romantic. The Libra female's intellect can be a little frightening to those who simply want a good time. Talk to her, accept the contradictory elements of her nature, and let her know how special she is.

Suggested Gifts A weekend away at a good hotel with excellent food; a sensual massage.

Charm to Charm a Libra Lover

~

Before performing the charm you'll need to find something that represents a bridge, or something with the Libra sigil on it. Friday is the best day; the best place is a well-kept garden or an old apple orchard. Wear shades of pale green, and carry a chrysoprase if possible.

Focus on your chosen object while thinking of the other person. Imagine a bridge being built between yourself and the other person, with a two-way flow of communication and ideas passing over it. Memorize this image, and call it to mind every time you are with the Libra.

Love Me at Last

Love me at last, or if you will not,
Leave me;
Hard words could never, as these half-
    words,
Grieve me:
Love me at last – or leave me.

Love me at last, or let the last word uttered
Be but your own;
Love me, or leave me – as a cloud, a vapor,
Or a bird flown.
Love me at last – I am but sliding water
Over a stone.

Alice Corbin late 19th century

SCORPIO IN LOVE

Man Dramatic, wickedly exciting, electrifying. The Scorpio male is possessive, but respects strength in others. He's also extremely attractive to others, so swallow your jealousy! Be adventurous, be loyal, and expect a thrilling (occasionally stormy) time . . .

Woman Fascinating, sensual, stimulating. The female Scorpio is secretive, needs to be in control, and has enormous will power. Be honest, emotionally open, and whatever you do, don't be possessive. Show her you're proud of her, but do be aware that the relationship may well be a little tempestuous.

Suggested Gifts Silk or velvet clothing (tasteful items, please!); a luxury cruise.

Charm to Intrigue your Scorpio

There is no particular "best day" to perform this charm, but the best time would be midnight. Wear black and dark red. Take a small representation of an eagle (a piece of jewelry, a little figurine, or – if you're lucky enough to have one – an eagle feather) to a lonely, deserted place; an actual desert is ideal (but please do make sure that you will be safe, wherever you decide).

Holding the symbol, envisage yourself becoming filled with controlled power, strength, and sheer determination – you'll need it if you plan a long-term relationship with a Scorpio! Carry it with you at all times to remind you of the qualities you need.

The Caution

Soft kisses may be innocent;
But ah! too easy maid, beware;
Tho' that is all thy kindness meant,
'Tis love's delusive, fatal snare.

Nor virgin e'er at first design'd
Thro' all the maze of love to stray;
But each new path allures her mind,
Till wandering on, she lose her way.

'Tis easy ere set out to stay;
But who the useful art can teach,
When sliding down a steepy way,
To stop, before the end we reach?

Keep ever something in thy power,
Beyond what would thy honour stain:
He will not dare to aim at more,
Who for small favours sighs in vain.

Catherine Cockburn 1679–1749

SAGITTARIUS IN LOVE

Man Outgoing, bold, adventurous, extravagant. The male Sagittarius needs to feel free — or at least not caged within a restrictive relationship. Be relaxed and optimistic with him, and you may find yourself on the journey of a lifetime.

Woman Restless, blunt, humorous, a good communicator. The Sagittarius female has a great love of the unknown and a sense of the magical qualities of life. Try to tie her down and she'll run a mile: share her adventures and you stand a good chance of a truly exciting and enlivening life.

Suggested Gifts Multi-blade penknife; waterproof, shockproof, multi-function watch.

Charm to Lure your Sagittarius

Thursday is the best day, and an airport or train station – or an ancient wood – the best place. Wear royal blue (something sporty or connected with travel is ideal) and slip a tumble-polished sodalite into your pocket. Take two small compasses with you: hold them side by side while saying mentally:

"[name], let me be your pole star. As this compass helps you on your quest through life, may it always bring you back to me."

If you want to be extravagant, buy compasses with metal covers, and have them engraved with your names. Keep your own and give the other to your Sagittarian – tell them it's for luck and they should always carry it with them!

To a Lady Making Love

~

Good madam, when ladies are willing,
A man must needs look like a fool;
For me I would not give a shilling
For one who would love out of rule.

You should leave us to guess by your
    blushing,
And not speak the matter so plain;
'Tis ours to write and be pushing,
'Tis yours to affect disdain.

That you're in a terrible taking,
By all these sweet oglings I see,
But the fruit that can fall without shaking,
Indeed is too mellow for me.
  Lady Mary Wortley Montagu 1689–1762

CAPRICORN IN LOVE

~

Man Single-minded, manipulative, pragmatic, ruthless. The Capricorn male often finds it difficult to express emotion, and needs to be the strong half of the partnership. Share his interests, but don't expect to be the most important thing in his life – and don't be too surprised if he leaves in pursuit of someone with more youth, wealth or social status (especially if you're strongly independent yourself)!

Woman Cautious, self-controlled, serious, reserved. In serious relationships, the Capricorn female tends to look for a good father rather than a lover. Treat her with respect, prove that you are a good provider, and don't expect her to share her secrets.

Suggested Gifts Shares in a large company; a lockable diary.

Charm to Entice a Capricorn

Saturday is the best day for this charm: the best places are mountains (especially near lakes), or a bank or the offices of a successful large company. Wear black.

You will need to take some money with you, a minimum of three coins – small denominations or old money are quite sufficient (if you wish to wear the charm afterwards, have holes drilled so you can mount the coins on discreet earrings, a neckchain or bracelet). Name the coins – one for you, one for your intended, and one for Fate: symbolically set Fate free (drop it near the building, bury it in the soil, or throw it into the water). Keep the other two coins safe.

We Who Have Loved

We who have loved, alas! may not be friends,
Too faint, or yet too fierce the stifled fire —
A random spark — and lo! our dread desire
Leaps into flame, as though to make
    amends
For chill, blank days, and with strange fury
    rends
The dying embers of Love's funeral pyre.
Electric, charged anew, the living wire
A burning message through our torpor
    sends.
Could we but pledge with loyal hearts and
    eyes
A friendship worthy of the fair, full past,
Now mutilate, and lost beyond recall,
Then might a Phoenix from its ashes rise
Fit for a soul flight; but we find, aghast,
Love must be nothing if not all in all.

Corinne Roosevelt Robinson late 19th century

AQUARIUS IN LOVE

~

Man Innovative, unusual, disconcerting. Friendship – and personal freedom – is usually more important than love to Aquarius. Maintain a strong sense of your own identity and worth, expect endless and fascinating discussions, and don't make emotional scenes.

Woman Inspiring, startling, unique, highly independent. The Aquarius female deals with all comers with integrity, and can be brutally honest. Don't expect blind devotion, or fidelity, and it might be best to be prepared for an unusual relationship . . .

Suggested Gifts A night out to see a top illusionist, followed by an all-night party; a kinetic sculpture or plasma globe.

Charm to Beguile an Aquarius

~

Your best course of action is to work on yourself. Sharpen your mind, read up on current affairs, find out which causes your intended lover supports and research them (and choose a few of your own!), develop a rational, cool approach to discussion. It's also important to build a strong wall around your own emotions — learn not to let the unflattering truth upset you, and curb your possessiveness or jealousy. Aquarians deal fairly with all people, but have great difficulty in expressing their deeper feelings, and will show their love by defending your point of view, or by taking care of you, rather than with flowers, anniversary cards or expressions of devotion.

The Constant Lover

~

Out upon it, I have loved
Three whole days together!
And am like to love three more,
If it hold fair weather.

Time shall moult away his wings
Ere he shall discover
In the whole wide world again
Such a constant lover.

But a pox upon't, no praise
There is due at all to me:
Love with me had made no stay,
Had it been any but she.

Had it any been but she,
And that very very face,
There had been at least ere this
A dozen dozen in her place.

Sir John Suckling 1609–41

PISCES IN LOVE

~

Man Unwilling to take responsibility, dreamy, vacillating. The male Pisces responds to harsh or continual demands by disappearing. He'll share your deepest secrets, dreams and fears — but don't try to tie him down . . .

Woman Unpredictable, imaginative, secretive. The Pisces female can never be "owned" — but she may allow you to share a little of the profound depths in which she lives. Never take her for granted. And never lie to her.

Suggested Gifts Something very personal — a handwritten love poem or hand-drawn picture; a walk along a deserted seashore (preferably in the Maldives!)

Charm to Enchant a Pisces

~

Thursday is the best day: a cliff overlooking the sea — or on a boat — is the best place. Wear turquoise clothing — and take an exotic seashell with you.

Sit and meditate on the shell, its shape, its color and texture: think about the animal it once housed, and its place of origin. Imagine what it would feel like to be an aquatic creature, flowing with the tides, exploring the mysterious depths of the oceans, free to travel the world without limitations: this gives you an insight into the Piscean psyche. Focus that extraordinary feeling of freedom and mystery into the shell, and keep it by your bed to help you connect with your beloved.

Last Sonnet

~

Bright Star! would I were steadfast as thou
   art —
Not in lone splendour hung aloft the
   night,
And watching, with eternal lids apart,
Like Nature's patient sleepless Eremite,
The moving waters at their priestlike task
Of pure ablution round earth's human
   shores,
Or gazing on the new soft-fallen mask
Of snow upon the mountains and the
   moors —
No — yet still steadfast, still unchangeable,
Pillow'd upon my fair love's ripening
   breast
To feel for ever its soft fall and swell,
Awake for ever in a sweet unrest;
Still, still to hear her tender-taken breath,
And so live ever — or else swoon to death.

John Keats 1795–1821

Plain as the Glistering Planets Shine

Plain as the glistering planets shine
When winds have cleaned the skies,
Her love appeared, appealed for mine,
And wantoned in her eyes.

Clear as the shining tapers burned
On Cytherea's shrine,
Those brimming, lustrous beauties turned,
And called and conquered mine.

The beacon-lamp that Hero lit
No fairer shone on sea,
No plainlier summoned will and wit,
Than hers encouraged me.

I thrilled to feel her influence near,
I struck my flag at sight.
Her starry silence smote my ear
Like sudden drums at night.

I ran as, at the cannon's roar,
The troops the ramparts man —
As in the holy house of yore
The willing Eli ran.

Here, lady, lo! that servant stands
You picked from passing men,
And should you need not heart nor hands
He bows and goes again.

Robert Louis Stevenson   1850–94

Chapter 6

~~❧~~

DREAM LOVER

Modern psychologists have joined ancient mystics in realizing the importance of our dreams. In view of the strength of the biological imperative of reproduction, it is not surprising that love and sex figure strongly in the dreams that reveal our subconscious mind, as well as in our waking thoughts.

The language of the subconscious is emotional rather than literal, and messages are couched in pictures rather than in words. In the dream world, the hat someone is wearing can be more important than the words they are saying!

Dreams and the images that clothe their secret truths may seem chaotic and random, but patient study can begin to unravel their mysteries, and it is well worth while keeping a dream diary — if nothing else, it will make fascinating reading on a rainy day!

Over the millennia, many researchers have sought to provide a dictionary of the language of dreams, and the following extracts from this continually evolving work have been chosen as being particularly relevant to deciphering subconscious hints and warnings about your love life.

It is important to realize however, that these dream definitions are suggested meanings only. The full interpretation of any dream is dependent both upon the atmosphere of the whole of the dream, and on the precise context in which the particular element appears.

Please note that the significance in dreams of many flowers and crystals can be derived from the meanings and uses of these items in the other sections of this book.

At the Mid Hour of Night

At the mid hour of night, when stars are
　　weeping, I fly
To the lone vale we loved, when life shone
　　warm in thine eye;
And I think that, if spirits can steal from the
　　region so fair
To revisit past scenes of delight, thou wilt
　　come to me there,
And tell me our love is remembered even in
　　the sky.

Then I sing the wild song it once was such
　　rapture to hear,
When our voices commingling breathed like
　　one on the ear;
And as Echo far off through the vale my sad
　　orison rolls,
I think O my love! 'tis thy voice from the
　　Kingdom of Souls
Faintly answering still the notes that once
　　were so dear.

Thomas Moore 1779–1852

DREAMS

~

Abandonment – to abandon someone you dislike, at the altar for example, is a sign of forthcoming prosperity. If you liked him or her, though, you will need inner strength to win through difficulties. If you were abandoned, then look out for an opportunity too good to miss.

Accident at sea – this indicates difficulties in your love life.

Admiration – if you were being admired then take care not to become complacent and vain!

Aisle of a church – think carefully before you commit yourself!

Allspice – romance.

Apple – if the fruit is sweet then romance is in the air, if sour then disappointment lurks nearby.

To Cloris

Cloris, I cannot say your Eyes
Did my unwary Heart surprise;
Nor will I swear it was your Face,
Your Shape, or any nameless Grace:
For you are so entirely Fair
To love a Part, Injustice were,
No drowning Man can know which Drop
Of water his last Breath did stop,
So when the Stars in Heaven appear,
And join to make the Night look clear,
The light we no one's Bounty call,
But the obliging Gift of all.
He that does Lips or Hands adore
Deserves them only, and no more;
But I love All, and every Part,
And nothing less can ease my Heart.
Cupid, that Lover weakly strikes,
Who can express what 'tis he likes.

Sir Charles Sedley   1639–1701

Archery – if you are unattached then prepare for attachment! Otherwise you may need strength to resist an alluring stranger.

Bark of a tree – be cautious in dealings with the opposite sex.

Basin or bowl – if full with anything but clean water then expect disappointment from your lover.

Bereavement – if of a complete stranger then expect news of an engagement or even a wedding – perhaps your own!

Butterfly – romantic success and family happiness.

Capsule – success in relationships, the more the merrier.

Car – parking signifies the end of a relationship.

Cards – King of Hearts is true love; Queen of Hearts is romance; Jack of Hearts is an infatuation.

Champagne – at a wedding, this signifies romance and joy.

Cloven hoof – traditionally a sign of an embarrassing deception.

Cockatoo – don't listen to gossip, but if you do then don't repeat it maliciously!

Collar – if dirty or disheveled then trust is misplaced, if clean and tidy then your heart is in safe hands.

Comb – losing a comb indicates the loss to a rival of a loved one.

Comet – a chance encounter that leads to love.

Cone – a powerful symbol that signifies sensual and sexual pleasure.

Corkscrew – beware of emotional entanglements.

On His Mistress, the Queen of Bohemia

You meaner beauties of the night,
That poorly satisfy our eyes
More by your number than your light,
You common people of the skies;
What are you when the moon shall rise?

You curious chanters of the wood,
That warble forth Dame Nature's lays,
Thinking your passions understood
By your weak accents; what's your praise,
When Philomel her voice shall raise?

You violets that first appear,
By your pure purple mantles known
Like the proud virgins of the year,
As if the spring were all your own;
What are you when the rose is blown?

So, when my mistress shall be seen
In form and beauty of her mind,
By virtue first, then choice, a Queen,
Tell me if she were not designed
Th' eclipse and glory of her kind.

Sir Henry Wotton 1568–1639

Crow – separation.

Cuckoo – misplaced trust.

Dancing couples – success in affairs of the heart.

Dice – if you are uncertain about a relationship, this dream image warns against simply trusting to luck for a happy ending.

Disgrace – curiously, the greater the disgrace the greater the success in love that is signified.

Donkey – sensual, sexual and even promiscuous liaisons are signified.

Dove – reciprocated love.

Drink – sweet drinks signify a passionate affair.

Duck and drake – romance.

Duet – romance and domestic bliss.

Ecstasy – an unsatisfying love life.

Like the Touch of Rain

~

Like the touch of rain she was
On a man's flesh and hair and eyes
When the joy of walking thus
Has taken him by surprise:

With the love of the storm he burns,
He sings, he laughs, well I know how,
But forgets when he returns
As I shall not forget her 'Go now'.

Those two words shut a door
Between me and the blessed rain
That was never shut before
And will not open again.

Edward Thomas 1878–1917

Elk – sexual activity.

Fingernails – long fingernails indicate that a relationship needs careful handling.

Fire – lighting a fire in a fireplace (or poking one) signifies sexual activity. Putting out a fire indicates that the fizz has gone out of a relationship.

Fireplace – if cold then dissatisfaction with a relationship is signified.

Flood – being swept away is a warning against misplacing your trust.

Florist – if you are unattached it indicates a new romance.

Freckles – you have admirers.

Gondola – a wish for romance.

Hammock – falling out is a warning not to take your partner for granted.

Hangover – beware of indiscretions.

Wild Nights – Wild Nights

~

Wild Nights – Wild Nights!
Were I with thee
Wild Nights should be
Our luxury!

Futile – the winds –
To a heart in port –
Done with the Compass –
Done with the Chart!

Rowing in Eden –
Ash, the Sea!
Might I but moor – Tonight –
In Thee!

Emily Dickinson   1830–86

Harem – sensual and sexual encounters are signified.

Hat – wearing a new hat indicates a new relationship; a hat that is too large warns of embarrassment; one that is too small signifies dissatisfaction.

Hedge – if verdant and lush then a successful love affair is signified.

Hothouse – a hothouse or conservatory, so long as it is in good condition, signifies an escalation of passion in a love affair.

Ice-skating — if with a partner, then beware of indiscretions.

Iguana — this is said to signify meeting unusual new friends...

Impotence — traditionally, this indicates an upsurge in activity in your love life.

Jungle — walking through one warns that an emotional entanglement is developing into a knotty problem!

Ketchup — a savory new friend.

Kitten — a frivolous affair.

Knot — untying a knot indicates the loosening of emotional bonds.

Why?

~

Why did you come, with your enkindled
     eyes
And mountain-look, across my lower way,
And take the vague dishonour from my day
By luring me from paltry things, to rise
And stand beside you, waiting wistfully
The looming of a larger destiny?

Why did you with strong fingers fling aside
The gates of possibility, and say
With vital voice the words I dream to-day?
Before, I was not much unsatisfied:
But since a god has touched me and
     departed,
I run through every temple, broken-
     hearted.

Mary Webb 1881–1927

Lace – you have admirers of the opposite sex.

Lane – walking along a narrow lane is a warning to be discreet.

Lantern – a swinging light warns against imprudence.

Lock – fitting a key into one signifies satisfaction with your love life.

Lute – to see or hear this instrument signifies light-hearted romance.

Magician – the resurrection of a long-past love affair.

Magnet – sexual magnetism and prowess.

Marble – this stone signifies turbulence in a love affair.

Mermaid – this is a personification of your love life and, therefore, whatever was happening around the mermaid is indicative of what is happening to your love life.

Metal – lead signifies disappointment in love. Any alloy either signifies a happy marriage or, if you are married already, a new child.

Moon – the full moon signifies success in all matters of love. If the moon is reflected in the water of a lake then the success will be particularly romantic and profound.

The Bargain

~

My true love hath my heart, and I have his,
By just exchange, one for the other given
I hold his dear, and mine he cannot miss,
There never was a better bargain driven.
His heart in me keeps me and him in one,
My heart in him his thoughts and senses
    guides;
He loves my heart, for once it was his own,
I cherish his, because in me it bides.
His heart his wound received from my sight,
My heart was wounded with his wounded
    heart;
For as from me on him his hurt did light,
So still methought in me his hurt did smart.
Both equal hurt, in this change sought our
    bliss:
My true love hath my heart and I have his.

Sir Philip Sidney 1554–86

Music – Deep and melodious organ music signifies sensuality and sexual satisfaction.

Musical instrument – carrying one which you do not play in waking life, signifies a fulfilling relationship.

Naked – in a public place, this signifies a break from routine and the chance to initiate a new relationship.

Name – if you can't remember your own name then take care that an illicit affair doesn't rob you of your reputation, your "good name."

Navel – the birth of a new affair of the heart.

Necklace — if beautiful, then the omens for a love affair are good.

Nightingale — either seen or heard, this bird is a herald of romance and domestic bliss.

Office — if it is the office where you work in your waking life, then it signifies that your love life is changing direction.

Omelet — if light and fluffy then an insubstantial but rapturous affair is signified.

Oyster — eating this shellfish signifies that a love affair is ripe for fulfillment.

Parachute — your trust is well placed (unless it failed to function properly, in which case your trust is *definitely* placed in the wrong hands).

Blest As the Immortal Gods Is He

~

Blest as the immortal gods is he,
The youth, who fondly sits by thee,
And hears and sees thee all the while
Softly speak and sweetly smile.

'Twas this deprived my soul of rest,
And raised such tumults in my breast;
For while I gazed, in transport tost,
My breath was gone, my voice was lost:

My bosom glowed; the subtle flame
Ran quick through all my vital frame,
O'er my dim eyes a darkness hung;
My ears with hollow murmurs rung.

In dewy damps my limbs were chilled;
My blood with gentle horror thrilled;
My feeble pulse forgot to play;
I fainted, sank, and died away.

Sappho   *600 BC approx.*

Park – enjoying a public park signifies a happy love life.

Parrot – this warns that you may be hurt by gossip about you.

Perfume – Musk signifies a passionate love affair. A light, delicate scent signifies a delightful romantic interlude.

Pickle – satisfaction.

Poetry – you are interesting to the opposite sex.

Ring – finding or being given a ring signifies a new relationship.

Sandals – a new romance.

Scarf – a new scarf indicates a new romance.

Scissors – the end of a relationship.

Shawl – worn over your head, this signifies satisfaction within a relationship.

Skein – tangled threads signify romantic disappointment, but if it is tidy then fulfillment in love is signified.

Song

A Scholar first my Love implor'd,
And then an empty, titled Lord;
The Pedant talk'd in lofty Strains;
Alas! his Lordship wanted Brains;
I list'ned not, to one or t'other,
But straight referr'd them to my Mother.

A Poet next my Love assail'd,
A lawyer hop'd to have prevail'd;
The Bard too much approv'd himself,
The Lawyer thirsted after Pelf:
I list'ned not, to one or t'other,
But still referr'd them to my Mother.

An Officer my Heart would storm,
A miser, sought me too, in Form;
But Mars was over-free and bold,
The Miser's Heart was in his Gold:
I list'ned not, to one or t'other,
Referring still unto my Mother.

And after them, some twenty more,
Successless were, as those before;
When Damon, lovely Damon, came!
Our hearts strait felt a mutual Flame;
I vow'd I'd have him, and no other,
Without referring to my Mother.

Dorothea Du Bois 1728–74

Sled – a roller coaster ride of an affair!

Snake – traditionally, serpents warn against false friends. Specifically, they warn you against taking lovers for granted.

Spire – true love.

Spring – when dreamed of out of season, this signifies a renewal of romantic activity.

Springs – these coiled wires etc. signify inconstancy.

Stag – sexual activity.

Stairs – falling up them signifies good luck in love.

Swan – domestic bliss and romantic happiness.

Tickling – beware of frivolity that leads to indiscretion.

Torch – a firebrand is a sign of an incandescent love affair.

A Lover's Plea

~

Shall I come, sweet Love, to thee,
When the evening beams are set?
Shall I not excluded be?
Will you find no feigned let?
Let me not, for pity, more
Tell the long hours at your door.

Who can tell what thief or foe
In the covert of the night
For his prey will work my woe,
Or through wicked foul despite?
So may I die unredressed,
Ere my long love be possessed.

But to let such dangers pass,
Which a lover's thoughts disdain,
'Tis enough in such a place
To attend love's joys in vain.
Do not mock me in thy bed,
While these cold nights freeze me dead.

Thomas Campion 1567–1620

Tree – planting a tree is a sign of being ready for a new relationship.

Unicorn – the blossoming of romance into commitment.

Vacuum cleaner – successful dealings with the opposite sex.

Valentine card – receiving one signifies turbulence in affairs of the heart, whereas giving one indicates you are ready for new relationships.

On Marriage *from* The Prophet
~

Then Almitra spoke again and said, And what
of Marriage, master?

And he answered saying:
You were born together, and together you
shall be for evermore.
You shall be together when the white wings
of death scatter your days.
Ay, you shall be together even in the silent
memory of God.
But let there be spaces in your
togetherness,
And let the winds of the heavens dance
between you.

Love one another, but make not a bond of
love:
Let it rather be a moving sea between the
shores of your souls.
Fill each other's cup but drink not from
one cup.

Give one another of your bread but eat not
   from the same loaf.
Sing and dance together and be joyous, but
   let each one of you be alone.
Even as the strings of a lute are alone
   though they quiver with the same music.
Give your hearts, but not into each other's
   keeping.
For only the hand of Life can contain your
   hearts.
And stand together yet not too near
   together:
For the pillars of the temple stand apart,
And the oak tree and the cypress grow not
   in each other's shadow.

Kahlil Gibran   1883–1931

Chapter 7

CRYSTAL MAGIC

Shakespeare said, "The course of true love never did run smooth . . ." and very often it's true. However, there are ways you can ease its progress. Try some of the following ideas and see what happens!

Shyness

~

It happens to nearly everyone. You've met someone to whom you are strongly attracted — but every time you find yourself in his/her presence you freeze up!

Take a good-sized piece of tiger's eye (for courage) and citrine (for eloquence). Grip them tightly between your hands, holding them at the level of your heart. Close your eyes, imagine the other person, and repeat to yourself, three times:

"I charge you, citrine and tiger's eye, to give me the courage to speak to [name], that I may discover his/her feeling for me."

Carry the stones with you whenever you know you will be in the other's presence, and to give the talismans extra energy, handle them while imagining his/her face. (You might find it helpful to sleep with the stones under your pillow, too.) If you prefer — and especially if shyness is a constant feature in your dealings with others — you could always wear the stones as jewelry: both gems are often found as rings or earrings.

To Cupid

~

Child, with many a childish wile,
Timid look, and blushing smile,
Downy wings to steal thy way,
Gilded bow, and quiver gay,
Who in thy simple mien would trace
The tyrant of the human race?
Who is he whose flinty heart
Hath not felt the flying dart?
Who is he that from the wound
Hath not pain and pleasure found?
Who is he that hath not shed
Curse and blessing on thy head?

Joanna Baillie 1762–1851

from The Art of Coquetry

~

First form your artful looks with studious
    care,
From mild to grave, from tender to severe.
Oft on the careless youth your glances
    dart,
A tender meaning let each glance impart.
Whene'er he meet your looks, with modest
    pride
And soft confusion turn your eyes aside,
Let a soft sigh steal out, as if by chance,
Then cautious turn, and steal another
    glance,
Caught by these arts, with pride and hope
    elate,
The destined victim rushes on his fate.

Charlotte Lennox 1720–1804

Passion

~

The first throes of love are usually a time when the rest of the world fades into insignificance and all that matters is your beloved – and what you do together . . . Fortunately, those in love are usually regarded with a smile and allowed a little more license than would otherwise be the case: these days, even employers are beginning to realize that happy workers are efficient workers!

However, to help you have the energy to cope both with your day-to-day life and the excitement of romance, try carrying a carnelian or a piece of red jasper. Keep it with you when you and your beloved are together, and take a moment or two to focus that glorious feeling of rapture and power into the stone.

Keep the stone with you in your normal daily life and work, and handle it every time you feel your concentration slipping. Remind yourself that the sooner you finish your appointed tasks, the sooner you can be together again: use the stone as a talisman to boost your performance in all things!

from Hero and Leander

It lies not in our power to love or hate
For will in us is over-ruled by fate.
When two are stripped, long ere the
    course begin,
We wish that one should lose, the other
    win;
And one especially do we affect
Of two gold ingots, like in each respect.
The reason no man knows; let it suffice,
What we behold is censured by our eyes.
Where both deliberate, the love is slight;
Who ever loved, that loved not at first
    sight?

Christopher Marlowe 1564–93

Oh Lift Me!

~

Oh lift me from the grass!
I die! I faint! I fail!
Let thy love and kisses rain
On my lips and eyelids pale.
My cheek is cold and white, alas!
My heart beats loud and fast: —
Oh! Press it to thine own again,
Where it will break at last.

Percy Bysshe Shelley 1792–1822

Tenderness

~

Hopefully, tender loving care will never be absent from your relationship. However, it does sometimes happen that your partner is less attentive and considerate than you'd like. Depending on the sort of person they are, you can make your point by reasoning with them, sulking loudly, flirting with everyone in sight, or going on strike . . .

However you choose to handle the situation, having a small crystal as a talisman may help. Choose moonstone (if you're female) or milky quartz (if you're male), clean the stone well and immerse it in a glass of mineral water. Leave the glass on your windowsill for a couple of hours (preferably in moonlight, and during the waxing moon is best). Take the stone from the water and hold it in your cupped hands, concentrating on the treatment you'd like from your partner: then consider what you could do for them in return. Try to think yourself inside your partner's mind, seeing things from their point of view. After all, your own behavior may not be improving the situation!

Drink the water, all the while thinking loving

thoughts toward your partner. Then hold the stone while you talk to them about your feelings — try to remain calm and non-accusatory. If you like, you could give them the crystal as a gift, but be sure they understand that it represents your wish for tenderness in the relationship.

The Good-Morrow

I wonder by my troth, what thou, and I
Did, till we lov'd? were we not wean'd till
 then?
But suck'd on country pleasures,
 childishly?
Or snorted we in the seven sleepers den?
'Twas so; But this, all pleasures fancies
 bee.
If ever any beauty I did see,
Which I desir'd, and got, 'twas but a
 dreame of thee.

And now good morrow to our waking
 soules,
Which watch not one another out of
 feare;
For love, all love of other sights
 controules,
And makes one little roome, an every
 where.
Let sea-discoverers to new worlds have
 gone,

Let Maps to other, worlds on worlds have
    showne,
Let us possesse one world, each hath one,
    and is one.

My face in thine eye, thine in mine
    appeares,
And true plaine hearts doe in the faces
    rest,
Where can we finde two better
    hemispheres
Without sharpe North, without declining
    West?
What ever dyes, was not mixt equally;
If our two loves be one, or, thou and I
Love so alike, that none doe slacken,
    none can die.

John Donne 1572–1631

Understanding

~

Understanding, forgiveness, acceptance, tolerance ... These are very often incredibly difficult things to feel, especially if you're feeling a little insecure and uncertain in yourself. Nevertheless they are essential if your relationship is to flourish — and that means you have to feel them about yourself as well as your partner.

It's often hard to forgive, and accept, ourselves as fallible humans, making mistakes and getting things wrong, especially when we're in love and want everything to be perfect.

Find a piece of turquoise — there's so much turquoise jewelry available you should be able to find something that appeals to you, but if not, buy (or be given) the raw material. As well as being a traditional spiritual stone, turquoise can, with concentration, allow you to delve into your own mind ...

Ideally, find somewhere high — a hillside, clifftop, the top floor of a high rise, the place matters less than the view. Compare the color of your stone to the sky; watch the clouds; feel your spirit rising above the earth, and soaring upwards ...

From far above, human concerns seem small and insignificant — or at least more in proportion! It's a lot easier to forgive yourself, and those you love, for foibles, mistakes and imperfections when you can fly high above them.

Of course, you need to come back to earth eventually, but bring your new perspective — and the turquoise that embodies it — back with you. Not an easy operation, but it will make you a far wiser, and far more attractive, individual!

from My Beloved Is Mine and I Am His

~

Nor Time, nor Place, nor Chance, nor
    Death can bow
My least desires unto the least remove;
He's firmly mine by Oath; I, His, by Vow;
He's mine by Faith, and I am His by Love;
He's mine by Water; I am His by Wine;
Thus I my Best-Beloved's am; thus He is
    mine.

He is my Altar; I, his Holy Place;
I am his Guest; and he, my living Food;
I'm his, by Penitence; He, mine by Grace;
I'm his, by Purchase; He is mine, by
    Blood;
He's my supporting Elm, and I, his Vine:
Thus I my Best-Beloved's am; thus He is
    mine.

He gives me wealth, I give him all my
    Vowes:
I give him songs; He gives me length of
    dayes:
With wreathes of Grace he crownes my
    conqu'ring brow
And I his Temples, with a Crowne of
    Praise,
Which he accepts as an ev'rlasting signe,
That I my Best-Beloved's am; that He is
    mine.

Francis Quarles 1592–1644

Happy Marriage

~

Thou genius of connubial love, attend!
Let silent wonder all thy powers suspend,
Whilst to thy glory I devote my lays,
And pour forth all my grateful heart in
    praise.
In lifeless strains let vulgar satire tell
That marriage oft is mixed with heaven
    and hell,
That conjugal delight is soured with
    spleen,
And peace and war compose the varied
    scene.
My muse a truth sublimer can assert,
And sing the triumphs of a mutual heart.

Thrice happy they who through life's
    varied tide
With equal pace and gentle motion glide,
Whom, though the wave of fortune sinks
    or swells,

One reason governs and one wish impels,
Whose emulation is to love the best,
Who feels no bliss but in each other blest,
Who knows no pleasure but the joys they
    give,
Nor cease to love but when they cease to
    live.
If fate these blessings in one lot combine,
Then let th'eternal page record them mine.

Thomas Blacklock   1721–91

Choosing

~

Making the right choice in romantic matters can be very difficult. How do you choose between several equally attractive people — especially if you are young and inexperienced?

To some extent, you need to trust your feelings, and any messages your subconscious — which normally has a good handle on what's what where people are concerned — might give you. However, you can give this a helping hand with a clear quartz double terminated crystal. While it can't make the choices for you, it can, with a little luck, help to steer you in the right direction.

You need to get to know your crystal. Study and explore it, until you know every flaw, facet and inclusion. Then sleep with it under your pillow — or in your hand — for five nights, writing down your dreams each morning.

Finally, take the crystal to a river or lake, and walk slowly along the bank. When you reach a spot that seems particularly pleasant, or interesting, stop for a while and look around you. Hold the crystal in your hand and gaze into it, repeating:

"Be with me in my choosing:

May your calm strength pass into me, that I may not err."

Your can repeat this formula whenever you need to. It's also a good idea to carry the crystal with you at all times.

Song

~

Stephon hath Fashion, Wit and Youth,
With all things else that please;
He nothing wants but Love and Truth
To ruin me with ease:
But he is flint, and beats the Art
To kindle fierce desire;
His pow'r inflames another's heart,
Yet he ne'er feels the fire.

O! how it does my soul perplex,
When I his charms recall,
To think he shou'd despise our Sex;
Or, what's worse, love 'em all!
My wearied heart, like Noah's Dove,
In vain has sought for rest;
Finding no hope to fix my Love,
Returns into my Breast.

Elizabeth Taylor 1685–1720

Giving

You think I give myself to you?
Not so, my friend, you do not see
My single purpose and intent –
To make you give myself to me.
Nora Cunningham late 19th century

Frivolity

~

Sometimes a new relationship can be a little too heavy, shutting out the rest of the world in favor of an intense, exclusive one-to-one, often centered on the bedroom. While this is fine in its place, it also means missing out on a lot of fun if it becomes a habit.

Buy yourself and your lover a piece of amethyst each (ones with rainbows are most effective – and probably the least expensive) – and then take them with you to a seriously silly place! Fun-fairs, carnivals, The Rocky Horror Show, a burlesque performance – whatever feels most appealing, as long as it is loud, manic and fun. Join in the spirit of the occasion: wear silly hats or noses, try a ride you've never tried before, throw peanuts at the actors (as long as you won't be thrown out), join in the choruses of the songs – just do something daft you'd never normally dream of doing. It's surprising how much of a release this can provide, and if nothing else, you'll feel closer from doing something silly together.

Try to channel the fun and frivolity of the experience into the crystals, so that handling them will bring back a sense of the excitement and pleasure you enjoyed together. Any time you feel things are becoming too oppressive, take your crystals for a day out (drag your partner along too!) and see if you can recapture that magic . . .

Upon Julia's Clothes

~

Whenas in silks my Julia goes,
Then, then, methinks, how sweetly flows
That liquefaction of her clothes!

Next, when I cast mine eyes and see
That brave vibration each way free,
– O how that glittering taketh me!

Robert Herrick 1591–1674

Remedia Amoris

~

Love, and the Gout invade the idle Brain,
Bus'ness prevents the Passion and the
    Pain:
Ceres and Bacchus, envious of our Ease,
Blow up the Flame, and heighten the
    Disease.
Withdraw the Fewel and the Fire goes out;
Hard Beds and Fasting, cure both Love
    and Gout.

Elizabeth Thomas 1675–1731

Stamina

~

There are times — bad patches, disappointments, financial or emotional troubles — when you simply need to be able to hang on and get through, somehow. Your own inner strength will pull you through most things, but sometimes you need a little extra boost.

Hematite — that beautiful, heavy, silvery black stone — is ideal as a talisman for such situations: not only does it, traditionally, deflect negativity, but it is also a very protective stone. If everything is going wrong in your love-life, take time out and obtain a large piece of hematite, and retire to a very solitary place (your own room if that's all that is available, although somewhere out of doors would be better).

Grip the stone tightly, focusing all your anxiety and uncertainty onto its shining surface — and imagine the stone shrugging off the problems with sublime confidence! Consider the good things in your life, then think about the ways you can improve — or, if there is no other option, escape from — the current situation.

It's very unlikely that you'll find an immediate solution, but at least you will have taken the first steps to resolving the problems — calm consideration of all the options open to you. Carry the hematite with you and handle it frequently, letting its cool solidity echo in your own actions, and borrowing its strength as you learn to deal with the unpleasant things of life!

Stanzas for Music

~

I speak not – I trace not – I breathe not thy
    name,
There is grief in the sound – there were
    guilt in the fame,
But the tear which now burns on my cheek
    may impart
The deep thought that dwells in that silence
    of heart.

Too brief for our passion, too long for our
    peace,
Were those hours, can their joy or their
    bitterness cease?
We repent – we abjure – we will break from
    our chain;
We must part – we must fly – to unite it
    again.

Oh! thine be the gladness and mine be the
    guilt,

Forgive me adored one – forsake if thou
  wilt;
But the heart which I bear shall expire
  undebased,
And man shall not break it – whatever thou
  mayst.

And stern to the haughty, but humble to
  thee,
My soul in its bitterest blackness shall be;
And our days seem as swift – and our
  moments more sweet,
With thee by my side – than the world at
  our feet.
One sight of thy sorrow – one look of thy
  love,
Shall turn me or fix, shall reward or
  reprove;
And the heartless may wonder at all we
  resign,
Thy lip shall reply not to them – but to
  mine.

   George Gordon, Lord Byron   1788–1824

Sometimes, no matter how hard you've worked at a relationship, or how much you want it to continue, the other person is no longer in love with you and wants to be set free. You could fight for them to stay, of course, but it's wiser, kinder, and ultimately healthier, to let them go.

However, this is often easier said than done, especially if you still love him/her. To make things a little less difficult, find a piece of amazonite or sodalite (or both), and keep them with you through the difficult time. They are both "feel good" stones, comforting to handle and attractive to look at; their colors are soothing and they may help you to feel a little more optimistic about life in general.

It's important, in such a situation, that you don't lose your sense of your own worth. This relationship may not have been successful, but there's no reason why the next one should go the same way, especially if you can learn from your mistakes. Keep the stone(s) with you to remind you that things aren't as gloomy as they might appear.

from Don Juan *Cantos 193 and 195*

~

I loved, I love you, for that love have lost
State, station, heaven, mankind's, my own
   esteem,
And yet cannot regret what it hath cost,
So dear is still the memory of that dream.
Yet if I name my guilt, 'tis not to boast;
None can deem harshlier of me than I
   deem.
I trace this scrawl because I cannot rest.
I've nothing to reproach or to request.

You will proceed in beauty and in pride,
Beloved and loving many. All is o'er
For me on earth, except some years to hide
My shame and sorrow deep in my heart's
   core.
These I could bear, but cannot cast aside
The passion which still rends it as before.
And so farewell – forgive me, love me – no,
That word is idle now, but let it go.

   George Gordon, Lord Byron   1788–1824

Dead Love

~

Oh never weep for love that's dead
Since love is seldom true
But changes his fashion from blue to red,
From brightest red to blue,
And love was born to an early death
And is so seldom true.

Then harbour no smile on your bonny face
To win the deepest sigh.
The fairest words on truest lips
Pass on and surely die,
And you will stand alone, my dear,
When wintry winds draw nigh.

Sweet, never weep for what cannot be,
For this God has not given.
If the merest dream of love were true
Then, sweet, we should be in heaven,
And this is only earth, my dear,
Where true love is not given.

Elizabeth Siddal 1834–62

Escape

~

Sometimes you yourself are the one who wants to be set free, especially from a restrictive or possessive partner (if he/she is also abusive or violent, it would be far better to get professional help rather than rely on talismans or books, no matter how well-meaning). Such a move takes willpower, determination and self-confidence: help the process along with serpentine, snowflake obsidian, or moss agate. Wearing the stone as jewelry is a good idea in this situation — that way you can keep it with you at all times — but if this isn't possible, try to find a comfortably large piece to carry with you. A "worry egg" would be highly appropriate; the egg shape represents undiscovered potential and new life.

As forcefully as you can, imagine yourself leading a different life, one that doesn't include the partner you're trying to leave, while holding the stone tightly. Will yourself to be strong, and not to let your lover induce you to stay. Convince yourself of your determination to start over by yourself, regardless of what he/she says. Then have the stone with you during what is bound to be an awkward confrontation . . .

Afterwards, handle the stone as much as you need to un-stress yourself – then start thinking about all the new experiences and people that will come your way!

The Way of It

~

This is the way of it, wide world over,
One is beloved, and one is the lover,
One gives and the other receives.
One lavishes all in a wild emotion,
One offers a smile for a life's devotion,
One hopes and the other believes,
One lies awake in the night to weep,
And the other drifts off in a sweet sound
    sleep.

One soul is aflame with a godlike passion,
One plays with love in an idler's fashion,
One speaks and the other hears.
One sobs, 'I love you,' and wet eyes show it,
And one laughs lightly, and says, 'I know it,'
With smiles for the other's tears.
One lives for the other and nothing beside,
And the other remembers the world is
    wide.

This is the way of it, sad earth over,
The heart that breaks is the heart of the
    lover,
And the other learns to forget.
'For what is the use of endless sorrow?
Though the sun goes down, it will rise to-
    morrow;
And life is not over yet.'
Oh! I know this truth, if I know no other,
That passionate Love is Pain's own mother.
        Ella Wheeler Wilcox 1850–1919

To his Coy Mistress

Had we but world enough, and time,
This coyness, Lady, were no crime.
We would sit down and think which way
To walk and pass our long love's day.
Thou by the Indian Ganges' side
Should'st rubies find: I by the tide
Of Humber would complain. I would
Love you ten years before the Flood,
And you should, if you please, refuse
Till the conversion of the Jews.
My vegetable love should grow
Vaster than empires, and more slow.
An hundred years should go to praise
Thine eyes and on thy forehead gaze;
Two hundred to adore each breast,
But thirty thousand to the rest.
An age at least to every part,
And the last age should show your heart.
For, Lady, you deserve this state,
Nor would I love at lower rate.

But at my back I always hear
Time's winged chariot hurrying near;
And yonder all before us lie
Deserts of vast eternity.
Thy beauty shall no more be found,
Nor, in my marble vault, shall sound
My echoing song: then worms shall try
That long preserved virginity,
And your quaint honour turn to dust,
And into ashes all my lust.
The grave's a fine and private place
But none, I think, do there embrace.
Now therefore, while the youthful hue
Sits on thy skin like morning dew,
And while thy willing soul transpires
At every pore with instant fires,
Now let us sport us while we may,
And now, like amorous birds of prey,
Rather at once our time devour
Than languish in his slow-chapt power.
Let us roll all our strength and all
Our sweetness up into one ball,
And tear our pleasures with rough strife

Through the iron gates of life:
Thus, though we cannot make our sun
Stand still, yet we will make him run.

Andrew Marvell 1621–78